lonely planet

ITALIAN
LAKES

ROAD
TRIPS

This edition written and researched by

**Cristian Bonetto, Belinda Dixon, Duncan Garwood,
Paula Hardy and Donna Wheeler**

HOW TO USE THIS BOOK

Reviews

In the Destinations section:

All reviews are ordered in our authors' preference, starting with their most preferred option. Additionally:

Sights are arranged in the geographic order that we suggest you visit them and, within this order, by author preference.

Eating and Sleeping reviews are ordered by price range (budget, midrange, top end) and, within these ranges, by author preference.

Map Legend

Routes
- Trip Route
- Trip Detour
- Linked Trip
- Walk Route
- Tollway
- Freeway
- Primary
- Secondary
- Tertiary
- Lane
- Unsealed Road
- Plaza/Mall
- Steps
-)= = Tunnel
- Pedestrian Overpass
- Walk Track/Path

Boundaries
- International
- State/Province
- Cliff

Hydrography
- River/Creek
- Intermittent River
- Swamp/Mangrove
- Canal
- Water
- Dry/Salt/ Intermittent Lake
- Glacier

Highway Markers
- A6 Autostrada
- SS231 State Highway
- SR203 Regional Highway
- SP3 Provincial Highway
- E74 Other Road

Trips
- 1 Trip Numbers
- 9 Trip Stop
- Walking tour
- Trip Detour

Population
- ☺ Capital (National)
- ◉ Capital (State/Province)
- ● City/Large Town
- ○ Town/Village

Areas
- Beach
- Cemetery (Christian)
- Cemetery (Other)
- Park
- Forest
- Reservation
- Urban Area
- Sportsground

Transport
- ✈ Airport
- Cable Car/ Funicular
- Ⓜ Metro station
- Ⓟ Parking
- Train/Railway
- Tram

Note: Not all symbols displayed above appear on the maps in this book

Symbols In This Book

- ✔ Top Tips
- Ⓢ Link Your Trips
- 💭 Tips from Locals
- ↱ Trip Detour
- 📖 History & Culture
- 👪 Family

- Food & Drink
- Outdoors
- Essential Photo
- Walking Tour
- Eating
- Sleeping

- ◉ Sights
- 🏖 Beaches
- 🏃 Activities
- 🎓 Courses
- ☞ Tours
- Festivals & Events

- 🛏 Sleeping
- Eating
- Drinking
- ☆ Entertainment
- Shopping
- ⓘ Information & Transport

These symbols and abbreviations give vital information for each listing:

- ☏ Telephone number
- ☺ Opening hours
- Ⓟ Parking
- ☺ Nonsmoking
- ❄ Air-conditioning
- @ Internet access
- 🛜 Wi-fi access
- 🏊 Swimming pool
- Vegetarian selection
- English-language menu
- Family-friendly

- Pet-friendly
- Bus
- Ferry
- Tram
- Train

- apt apartments
- d double rooms
- dm dorm beds
- q quad rooms
- r rooms
- s single rooms
- ste suites
- tr triple rooms
- tw twin rooms

CONTENTS

Walkway over Lake Como, Varenna (p76)

WELCOME TO
THE
ITALIAN LAKES

From the snowy slopes of the alpine Milky Way region to villas framed by gazebos and mould-breaking art and architecture, northern Italy is as action-packed as it is artful. The glacial lakes of Lombardy – where fishing boats bob in tiny harbours while palaces float in the Borromean Gulf – have been a popular spot since Roman times. Meanwhile, artists, celebrities and moneyed Mitteleuropeans have been lured here since the days of the Grand Tour, by world-class art, an embarrassment of culinary riches, cult wines and a slew of sophisticated cities.

While Venice's city of palaces dazzles and Milan's Golden Quad rapidly helps to relieve you of your hard-earned cash, you're never far from a rural hinterland that still moves with the rhythm of the seasons and seems largely untouched by modern tourism.

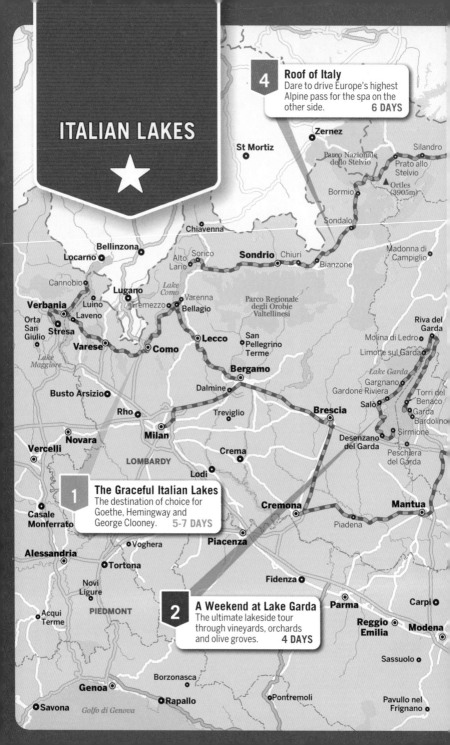

ITALIAN LAKES

★

4 **Roof of Italy**
Dare to drive Europe's highest Alpine pass for the spa on the other side. **6 DAYS**

1 **The Graceful Italian Lakes**
The destination of choice for Goethe, Hemingway and George Clooney. **5-7 DAYS**

2 **A Weekend at Lake Garda**
The ultimate lakeside tour through vineyards, orchards and olive groves. **4 DAYS**

AUSTRIA

Fortezza   Brunico

Bressanone

Merano

Ortisei

Bolzano

Cornaiano

Marmolada
(3343m)

Predazzo

San Michele   TRENTINO-
all'Adige   ALTO
                ADIGE

Trento   Feltre   Belluno

                            Vittorio
                            Veneto

                            Conegliano

Rovereto   Pordenone

                Bassano   VENETO
                del Grappa   Oderzo
        Thiene Montebelluna

Valdagno   Portogruaro

                Castelfranco   Treviso
                Veneto

Vicenza   San Donà
                                        di Piave

Verona Soave   Mestre

        Monteforte   Venice
        d'Alpone   Padua   Lido di
                            Venezia

                Este   Chioggia

        Legnago

                        Rovigo

Ostiglia

                                Po
                                Delta

        Ferrara

                        Comacchio

        Argenta   Valle di
                            Comacchio

    Bologna

Imola   Ravenna

FRIULI
VENEZIA
GIULIA

Udine

Monfalcone

Lignano
Sabbiadoro

Grado

Golfo di
Trieste

3 Northern Cities
Visit grand-slam cultural sites
amid the rice paddies of the
Po Valley.   **7-10 DAYS**

N 0   50 km
   0   25 miles

ITALIAN LAKES
HIGHLIGHTS

★

Lake Como (left)
The most picturesque of the region's lakes, Lake Como has long been a lure for the rich and famous. See it on Trip 1

Venice (above)
This unique and hauntingly beautiful city needs no introduction. See it on Trip 3

Sirmione (right)
Jutting out onto Lake Garda, Sirmione astounds with its Roman ruins, spectacular views and thermal spring. See it on Trip 2

Duomo di Milano (Milan Cathedral), p54

MILAN

Home of Italy's stock exchange, an industrial powerhouse and the internationally accepted arbiter of taste in fashion and design, Milan is a seething metropolis. At times it can seem brash and soulless but beneath the veneer is a serious sense of history and place.

Getting Around

It simply isn't worth having a car in Milan. You're better off using public transport; a ticket costs €1.50 and is valid for one metro ride or up to 90 minutes on buses and trams. Route maps are available from ATM Info points, or download the IATM app.

Parking

In the centre, street parking costs €1.50 per hour in the city centre. To pay, buy a SostaMilano card from a tobacconist, scratch off the date and hour, and display it on your dashboard. Underground car parks charge between €25 and €40 for 24 hours.

Discover the Taste of Milan

Internal Italian immigrants have injected the cuisine of virtually every region into the lifeblood of the city, where you'll also find Lombard classics alongside a rich international selection of anything from Ethiopian to sushi. Milan's clutch of Michelin-starred chefs cook up some of Italy's most sophisticated food.

Where to Stay

The tourist office distributes *Milano Hotels*, a free annual listings guide to Milan's 350 plus hotels. Good value is difficult to come by in most budget ranges, and downright impossible during large fairs. That said, booking ahead and comparison-shopping online for 'special rates' can result in unexpected deals.

Useful Websites

Cenacolo Vinciano (www.cenacolovinciano.org) Booking for *The Last Supper*.

Milano da Bere (www.milanodabere.it) Events, dining and drinking.

Milan Is Tourism (www.turismo.milano.it) Milan's city website.

Road Trip through Milan: 3

Destinations coverage: p54

Traditional gondola on a Venetian canal

VENICE

A magnificent, unforgettable spectacle, Venice (Venezia) is a hauntingly beautiful city. For 1000 years it was one of Europe's great sea powers and its unique cityscape reflects this, with golden Byzantine domes and great Gothic churches, noble *palazzi* and busy waterways.

Getting Around

Venice is off-limits to cars, leaving you to walk or take a boat. You'll inevitably get lost at some point but directions to Piazza San Marco, the Rialto and Accademia are posted on yellow signs. *Vaporetti* (small ferries) ply the city's waterways; a one-way ticket costs €7.

Parking

Once you've crossed the Ponte della Libertà bridge from Mestre, you'll have to park at Piazzale Roma or Tronchetto car parks; bank on up to €26 for 24 hours.

Discover the Taste of Venice

Venice's version of tapas, bar snacks called *cicheti* are served in *osterie* across town at lunch and between 6pm and 8pm.

Live Like a Local

Many Venetians open their historical homes as B&Bs – check the Turismo Venezia website for lists. Dorsoduro and San Polo are charming areas to stay in, near major museums and with plenty of bar action. Cannaregio is another good option, relatively untouristy and in parts very picturesque.

Useful Websites

A Guest in Venice (www.unospitedivenezia.it) Hotelier association that provides information on upcoming exhibits, events and lectures.

Turismo Venezia (www.turismovenezia.it) The city's official tourism site.

Veneto Inside (www.venetoinside.com) Book entry to the Basilica di San Marco, guided visits and water taxis.

Road Trip through Venice: 3

Destinations coverage: p90

11

NEED TO KNOW

CURRENCY
Euros (€)

LANGUAGE
Italian

VISAS
Generally not required for stays of up to 90 days (or at all for EU nationals); some nationalities need a Schengen visa (p128).

FUEL
You'll find filling stations on autostradas and all major roads. The price of fuel can be higher in Italy than in neighbouring countries; be sure to check before you go.

RENTAL CARS
Avis (www.avis.com)

Europcar (www.europcar.com)

Hertz (www.hertz.com)

Maggiore (www.maggiore.it)

IMPORTANT NUMBERS
Ambulance (☎118)

Emergency (☎112)

Police (☎113)

Roadside Assistance (☎803 116; ☎800 116800 from a foreign mobile phone)

Climate

Dry climate
Warm to hot summer, mild winter
Warm to hot summer, cold winter
Mild summer, cold winter
Cold climate

Milan
GO Dec–Mar (skiing) & Sep

Venice
GO Feb–Mar & Sep–Nov

When to Go

High Season (Jul & Aug)
» Prices high on the coast; accommodation discounts available in some cities in August.

» Prices rocket for Christmas, New Year and Easter.

» Late December to March is high season in the Alps and Dolomites.

Shoulder Season (Apr–Jun & Sep–Oct)
» Good deals on accommodation, especially in the south.

» Spring is best for festivals, flowers and local produce.

» Autumn provides warm weather and the grape harvest.

Low Season (Nov–Mar)
» Prices at their lowest – up to 30% less than in high season.

» Many sights and hotels closed in coastal and mountainous areas.

» A good period for cultural events in large cities.

Daily Costs

Budget: Less than €100
» Double room in a budget hotel: €50–100
» Pizza or pasta: €6–12
» Excellent markets and delis for self-catering

Midrange: €100–200
» Double room in a midrange hotel: €80–180
» Lunch and dinner in local restaurants: €25–45
» Museum admission: €5–15

Top End: More than €200
» Double room in a four- or five-star hotel: €200–450
» Top-restaurant dinner: €50–150
» Opera tickets: €15–150

Eating

Restaurants (Ristoranti) Formal service and refined dishes, with prices to match.

Trattorias Family-run places with informal service and classic regional cooking.

Vegetarians Most places offer good vegetable starters and side dishes.

Price indicators for a meal with *primo* (first course), *secondo* (second course), *dolce* (dessert) and a glass of house wine:

€	less than €25
€€	€25–45
€€€	more than €45

Sleeping

Hotels From luxury boutique palaces to modest family-run *pensioni* (small hotels).

B&Bs Rooms in restored farmhouses, city *palazzi* (mansions) or seaside bungalows.

Agriturismi Farmstays range from working farms to luxury rural retreats.

Price indicators for a double room with bathroom:

€	less than €100
€€	€100–200
€€€	more than €200

Arriving in Italy

Leonardo da Vinci (Fiumicino) Airport (Rome)
Rental cars Agencies are near the multilevel car park. Look for signs in the Arrivals area.

Trains & buses Run every 30 minutes from 6.30am to 11.40pm.

Night buses Hourly departures from 12.30am to 5am.

Taxis Set fare €48; 45 minutes.

Malpensa Airport (Milan)
Rental cars In Terminal 1 agencies are on the 1st floor; in Terminal 2 in the Arrivals hall.

Malpensa Express & Shuttle Runs every 30 minutes from 5am to 11pm.

Night buses Limited services from 12.15am to 5am.

Taxis Set fare €90; 50 minutes.

Capodichino Airport (Naples)
Rental cars Agencies are located in the main Arrivals hall.

Airport shuttles Run every 20 minutes from 6.30am to 11.40pm.

Taxis Set fare €19 to €23; 30 minutes.

Mobile Phones (Cell Phones)

Local SIM cards can be used in European, Australian and unlocked, multiband US phones. Other phones must be set to roaming.

Internet Access

Wi-fi is available in many lodgings and city bars, often free. Internet cafes are thin on the ground and typically charge €2 to €6 per hour.

Money

ATMs at airports, most train stations and in towns and cities. Credit cards accepted in most hotels and restaurants. Keep cash for immediate expenses.

Tipping

Not obligatory but round up the bill in pizzerias and trattorias; 10% is normal in upmarket restaurants.

Useful Websites

Italia (www.italia.it) Official tourism site.

Michelin (www.viamichelin.it) A useful route planner.

Agriturismi (www.agriturismi. it) Guide to farmstays.

Lonely Planet (www. lonelyplanet.com/italy) Destination lowdown.

For more, see Italy Driving Guide (p115).

Road Trips

1 The Graceful Italian Lakes 5-7 Days
The destination of choice for Goethe, Hemingway and George Clooney. (p17)

2 A Weekend at Lake Garda 4 Days
The ultimate lakeside tour through vineyards, orchards and olive groves. (p29)

3 Northern Cities 7-10 Days
Visit grand-slam cultural sites amid the rice paddies of the Po Valley. (p37)

4 Roof of Italy 6 Days
Dare to drive Europe's highest Alpine pass for the spa on the other side. (p45)

Highway on the western shore of Lake Garda (p29)
JORG GREUEL/GETTY IMAGES ©

The Graceful Italian Lakes

1

Writers from Goethe to Hemingway have lavished praise on the Italian lakes, dramatically ringed by snow-powdered mountains and garlanded by grand villas and exotic, tropical flora.

TRIP HIGHLIGHTS

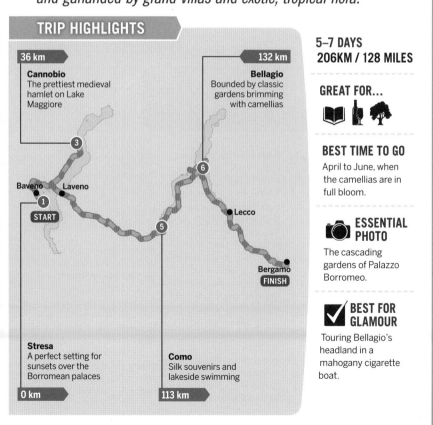

36 km

Cannobio
The prettiest medieval hamlet on Lake Maggiore

132 km

Bellagio
Bounded by classic gardens brimming with camellias

Baveno

Laveno

START

Lecco

Bergamo
FINISH

Stresa
A perfect setting for sunsets over the Borromean palaces

0 km

Como
Silk souvenirs and lakeside swimming

113 km

5–7 DAYS
206KM / 128 MILES

GREAT FOR...

BEST TIME TO GO
April to June, when the camellias are in full bloom.

ESSENTIAL PHOTO
The cascading gardens of Palazzo Borromeo.

BEST FOR GLAMOUR
Touring Bellagio's headland in a mahogany cigarette boat.

Left View of Lake Como from Villa Monastero (p24)

1

The Graceful Italian Lakes

Formed at the end of the last ice age, and a popular holiday spot since Roman times, the Italian lakes have an enduring natural beauty. At Lake Maggiore (Lago Maggiore) the palaces of the Borromean Islands lie like a fleet of fine vessels in the gulf, their grand ballrooms and shell-encrusted grottoes once host to Napoleon and Princess Diana, while the siren call of Lake Como (Lago di Como) draws Arabian sheikhs and Hollywood movie stars to its discreet forested slopes.

1 Stresa (p66)

More than Como and Garda, Lake Maggiore has retained the belle époque air of its early tourist heyday. Attracted by the mild climate and the easy access the new 1855 railway provided, the European *haute bourgeoisie* flocked to buy and build grand lakeside villas.

The star attractions are the Borromean Islands (Isole Borromee) and their palaces. **Isola Bella** took the name of Carlo III's wife, the *bella* Isabella, in the 17th century, when its centrepiece, **Palazzo Borromeo** (✆0323 3 05 56; www.isoleborromee. it; Isola Bella; adult/child €15/8.50, incl Palazzo Madre €21/10; ✆9am-5.30pm mid-Mar–mid-Oct), was built. Construction of the villa and gardens was thought out in such a way that the island would have the appearance of a vessel, with the villa at the prow and the gardens dripping down 10 tiered terraces at the rear. A separate €4 ticket gives you access to the **Galleria dei Quadri** (Picture Gallery), where Old Masters, including Rubens, Titian and Veronese, adorn the walls.

By contrast, **Isola Madre** eschews ostentation for a more romantic, familial

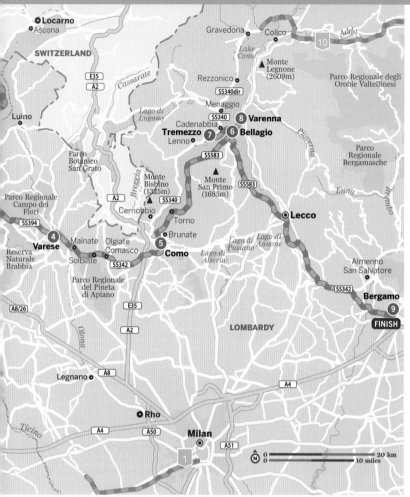

atmosphere. The 16th- to 18th-century **Palazzo Madre** (☏0323 3 05 56; www.isoleborromee.it; adult/child €12/6.50, incl Palazzo Borromeo €21/10; ⏱9am-5.30pm mid-Mar–mid-Oct) includes a 'horror' theatre with a cast of devilish marionettes, while Chinese pheasants stalk the English gardens.

LINK YOUR TRIP

4 Roof of Italy

From Como take the SS340 to Gravedona from where you plunge eastwards into the Valtellina vineyards and over the Alps to Merano (p45).

The Drive » Leave Stresa eastwards on the Via Sempione (SS33) skirting the edge of the lake for this short, 14km drive. Pass through Baveno and round the eastern edge of the gulf through the greenery of the Fondo Toce natural reserve. When you reach the junction with the SS34, turn right for Verbania.

❷ Verbania (p68)

The late-19th-century **Villa Taranto** (☎032355 66 67; www.villataranto.it; Via Vittorio Veneto 111, Verbania Pallanza; adult/reduced €10/5.50; ⏰8.30am-6.30pm mid-Mar–Sep, 9am-4pm Oct) sits just outside Verbania. In 1931, royal archer and Scottish captain Neil McEacharn bought the villa from the Savoy family and started to plant some 20,000 species. With its rolling hillsides of purple rhododendrons and camellias, acres of tulip flowers and hothouses full of equatorial lilies it is considered one of Europe's finest botanical gardens. During the last week in April, **Settimana del Tulipano** takes place, when tens of thousands of tulips erupt in magnificent multicoloured bloom.

The Drive » Pick up the SS34 again, continuing in a northeasterly direction out of Verbania, through the suburbs of Intra and Pallanza. Once you've cleared the town the 20km to Cannobio are the prettiest on the tour, shadowing the lakeshore the entire way with views across the water.

TRIP HIGHLIGHT

❸ Cannobio (p69)

Sheltered by a high mountain and sitting at the foot of the Cannobino valley, the medieval hamlet of Cannobio is located 5km from the Swiss border. **Piazza di Vittorio Emanuele III**, lined with pastel-hued houses, is the location of a huge Sunday market that attracts visitors from Switzerland. Right in the heart of the historic centre, in a 15th-century monastery that later became the home of the Pironi family, is the atmospheric **Hotel Pironi** (☎0323 7 06 24; www.pironihotel.it; Via Marconi 35; s €120, d €150-195, tr €185-230; 🅿🛜♿). Behind its thickset walls are rooms with frescoed vaults, exposed timber beams and an assortment of tastefully decorated bedrooms.

You can hire small **sailing boats** (€120 per day) and make an excursion to the ruined **Castelli della Malpaga**, located on two rocky islets to the south of Cannobio. In summer it is a favourite picnic spot.

Alternatively, explore the wild beauty of the Valle Cannobina up the SP75, following the surging Torrente Cannobino stream into the heavily wooded hillsides to Malesco. Just 2.5km along the valley, in Sant'Anna, the torrent forces its way powerfully through a narrow gorge known as the **Orrido di Sant'Anna**, crossed at its narrowest part by a Romanesque bridge.

The Drive » The next part of the journey involves retracing the previous 22km drive to Verbania-Intra to board the cross-lake ferry to Laveno. Ferries run every 20 minutes (one-way tickets cost €7 to

---

↱ DETOUR: LAGO D'ORTA

Start: ❶ Stresa

Separated from Lake Maggiore by Monte Mottarone (1492m) and enveloped by thick, dark-green woodlands, Lago d'Orta would make a perfect elopers' getaway. At 13.4km long by 2.5km wide you can drive around the lake in a day. The focal point is the captivating medieval village of **Orta San Giulio**, which sits across from Isola San Giulio where you'll spy the frescoed, 12th-century **Basilica di San Giulio** (p69). Come during the week and you'll have the place largely to yourself.

€11.60 for car and driver). Once in Laveno pick up the SS233 and then the SS394 for the 23km drive to Varese.

- - - - - - - - - -

➍ Varese

Spread out to the south of the Campo dei Fiori hills, Varese is a prosperous provincial capital. From the 17th century onwards, Milanese nobles began to build second residences here, the most sumptuous being the **Palazzo Estense**, completed in 1771 for Francesco III d'Este, the governor of the Duchy of Milan. Although you cannot visit the palace you are free to wander the vast Italianate **gardens** (⊗8am-dusk).

To the north of the city sits another great villa, **Villa Panza** (☎0332 28 39 60; Piazza Litta 1; adult/reduced €8/3; ⊗10am-6pm Tue-Sun), donated to the state in 1996. Part of the donation were 150 contemporary canvases collected by Giuseppe Panza di Biumo, mostly by post-WWII American artists. One of the finest rooms is the 1830 **Salone Impero** (Empire Hall), with heavy chandeliers and four canvases by David Simpson (born in 1928).

The Drive » The 28km drive from Varese to Como isn't terribly scenic, passing through a string of small towns and suburbs nestled in the wooded hills. The single-lane SS342 passes through Malnate, Solbiate and Olgiate Comasco before reaching Como.

- - - - - - - - - -

TRIP HIGHLIGHT

➎ Como (p71)

Built on the wealth of its silk industry, Como is an elegant town and remains Europe's most important producer of silk products. The **Museo della Seta** (Silk Museum; ☎031 30 31 80; www.museosetacomo.com; Via Castelnuovo 9; adult/reduced €10/7; ⊗10am-6pm Tue-Fri, to 1pm Sat) unravels the town's industrial history, with early dyeing and printing equipment on display. At **A Picci** (p73) you can buy top-quality scarves, ties and fabrics for a fraction of the cost you'd pay elsewhere.

After wandering the medieval alleys of the historic centre take a stroll along **Passeggiata Lino Gelpi**, where you pass a series of waterfront mansions, finally arriving at **Villa Olmo** (☎031 25 23 52; Via Cantoni 1; gardens free, villa

LAGO MAGGIORE EXPRESS

The **Lago Maggiore Express** (www.lagomaggiore express.com; adult/child €32/16) is a picturesque day trip you can do without the car. It includes train travel from Arona or Stresa to Domodossola, from where you get the charming *Centovalli* train, crossing 100 valleys, to Locarno in Switzerland and a ferry back to Stresa. The two-day version is perhaps better value if you have the time, costing €40/20 per adult/child.

entry varies by exhibition; ⊗villa during exhibitions 9am-12.30pm & 2-5pm Mon-Sat, gardens 7.30am-11pm summer, to 7pm winter). Set grandly facing the lake, this Como landmark was built in 1728 by the Odescalchi family, related to Pope Innocent XI, and now hosts blockbuster art shows. During the summer the **Lido di Villa Olmo** (71), an open-air swimming pool and lakeside bar, is open to the public.

On the other side of Como's marina, the **Funicolare Como-Brunate** (p71) whisks you uphill to the quiet village of **Brunate** for splendid views across the lake.

The Drive » The 32km drive from Como to Bellagio along the SS583 is spectacular. The narrow road swoops and twists around the lake shore the entire way and rises up out of Como giving panoramic views over the lake. There are plenty of spots en route where you can pull over for photographs.

WHY THIS IS A CLASSIC TRIP
PAULA HARDY, AUTHOR

Despite centuries of fame as a tourist destination, there's a timeless glamour to the Italian lakes, especially Lake Como with its mountainous amphitheatre of snow-capped Alps. One of the best ways to see it is to walk the old mule tracks. There are some easy walks with fabulous views around Brunate. Pick up a map showing the trails from the Como tourist office.

Top: Villa Melzi D'Eril, Bellagio
Left: Gardens of Palazzo Borromeo, Stresa (p18)
Right: Wisterias hang over Lake Como

TRIP HIGHLIGHT

❻ Bellagio (p74)

It's impossible not to be charmed by Bellagio's waterfront of bobbing boats, its maze of stone staircases, cypress groves and showy gardens.

Villa Serbelloni (☎031 95 15 55; Piazza della Chiesa 14; adult/child €9/5; ⊘ tours 11.30am & 2.30pm Tue-Sun mid-Mar–Oct) covers much of the promontory on which Bellagio sits. Although owned by the Rockefeller Foundation, you can still tour the gardens on a guided tour. Otherwise stroll the grounds of neoclassical **Villa Melzi d'Eril** (☎339 4573838; www. giardinidivillamelzi.it; Lungo Lario Manzoni; adult/reduced €6.50/4; ⊘9.30am-6.30pm Apr-Oct), which run right down to the lake and are adorned with classical statues couched in blushing azaleas.

Barindelli (☎338 211 0337; www.barindellitaxiboats. com; Piazza Mazzini) operates slick, mahogany cigarette boats in which you can tool around the headland for a sunset tour (€130, seats 10).

The Drive ❯❯ The best way to reach Tremezzo, without driving all the way around the bottom of the lake, is to take the ferry from Piazza Mazzini. One-way fares cost €2, but for sightseeing you may want to consider the one-day central lake ticket, covering Bellagio, Varenna, Tremezzo and Cadenabbia, for €12.

❼ Tremezzo (p75)

Tremezzo is high on everyone's list for a visit to the 17th-century **Villa Carlotta** (☎034 44 04 05; www.villacarlotta.it; Via Regina 2; adult/reduced €9/7; ⏰9am-7.30pm Apr–mid-Oct), whose botanic gardens are filled with orange trees knitted into pergolas and some of Europe's finest rhododendrons, azaleas and camellias. The villa, which is strung with paintings and fine alabaster-white sculptures (especially fine are those by Antonio Canova), takes its name from the Prussian princess who was given the palace in 1847 as a wedding present from her mother.

The Drive » As with the trip to Tremezzo, the best way to travel to Varenna is by ferry from Piazza Mazzini, in Bellagio.

❽ Varenna (p76)

Wander the flower-laden pathway from Piazzale Martiri della Libertà to the gardens of **Villa Cipressi** (p76), now a luxury hotel (singles €110 to €140, doubles €140 to €190), and, 100m further south, **Villa Monastero** (☎034 29 54 50; www.villamonastero.eu; Via IV Novembre; villa & gardens adult/reduced €8/4, gardens only €5/2; ⏰gardens 9.30am-7pm, villa 9.30am-7pm Fri-Sun Mar-Jul & Sep, daily Aug), a

Varenna shines over Lake Como

former convent turned into a vast residence by the Mornico family in the 17th century. In both cases, you can stroll through the verdant gardens admiring magnolias, camellias and exotic yuccas.

The Drive ⟫ Departing Bellagio, pick up the SS583, but this time head southeast towards Lecco down the other 'leg' of Lake Como. As with the stretch from Como to Bellagio, the road hugs the lake, offering spectacular views the whole 20km to Lecco. Once you reach Lecco head south out of town down Via Industriale and pick up the SS342 for the final 30km to Bergamo.

9 Bergamo (p81)

Although Milan's skyscrapers are visible on a clear day, historically Bergamo was more closely associated with Venice (Venezia). Hence the elegant Venetian-style architecture of **Piazza Vecchia**, considered by Le Corbusier to be 'the most beautiful square in Europe'. The **Palazzo della Ragione** (adult/reduced €5/3; ⊘10am-9pm Tue-Sun Jun-Sep, 9.30am-5.30pm Mon-Fri, 10am-6pm Sat & Sun Oct-Apr) was the seat of medieval city governance.

Behind this secular core sits the **Piazza del Duomo**, with its modest baroque **cathedral** (p83). A great deal more interesting is the **Basilica di Santa Maria Maggiore** (Piazza del Duomo; ⊘9am-12.30pm & 2.30-6pm Apr-Oct, shorter hours Nov-Mar) **next door. To its whirl of** frescoed, Romanesque apses, begun in 1137, Gothic touches were added as was the Renaissance **Cappella Colleoni** (⊘9am-12.30pm & 2-6.30pm Mar-Oct, 9am-12.30pm & 2-4.30pm Tue-Sun Nov-Feb), **the mausoleum-cum-chapel of the famous mercenary commander, Bartolomeo Colleoni (1696–1770). Demolishing an entire apse of the basilica, he commissioned Giovanni Antonio Amadeo to create a tomb that is now considered a masterpiece of Lombard art with its exuberant rococo frescoes by Giambattista Tiepolo.**

SEAPLANES ON THE LAKE

For a touch of Hollywood glamour, check out **Aero Club Como** (www.lagomaggioreexpress.com), who has been sending seaplanes out over the lakes since 1930. The 30-minute flight to Bellagio from Como costs €140 for two people. Longer excursions over Lake Maggiore are also possible. In summer you need to reserve at least three days in advance.

Ceiling of the Duomo di Bergamo (Bergamo Cathedral, p83)

A Weekend at Lake Garda

2

Poets, politicians, divas and dictators, they've all been drawn to glorious Lake Garda with mountains to the north, vine-clad hills to the south and a string of medieval towns encircling its shores.

TRIP HIGHLIGHTS

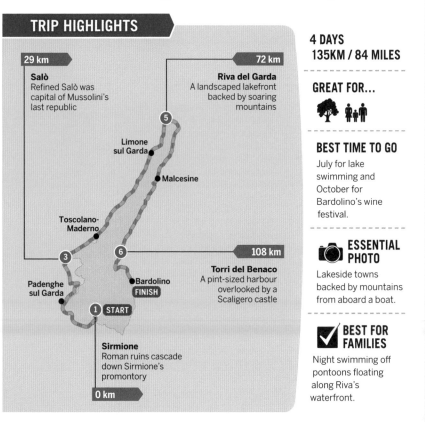

29 km

Salò
Refined Salò was capital of Mussolini's last republic

72 km

Riva del Garda
A landscaped lakefront backed by soaring mountains

5

Limone sul Garda

Malcesine

Toscolano-Maderno

3

6

108 km

Torri del Benaco
A pint-sized harbour overlooked by a Scaligero castle

Padenghe sul Garda

Bardolino
FINISH

1 **START**

Sirmione
Roman ruins cascade down Sirmione's promontory

0 km

4 DAYS
135KM / 84 MILES

GREAT FOR...

BEST TIME TO GO

July for lake swimming and October for Bardolino's wine festival.

ESSENTIAL PHOTO

Lakeside towns backed by mountains from aboard a boat.

BEST FOR FAMILIES

Night swimming off pontoons floating along Riva's waterfront.

A Weekend at Lake Garda

At 370 sq km Lake Garda (Lago di Garda) is the largest of the Italian lakes, straddling the border between Lombardy and the Veneto. Vineyards, olive groves and citrus orchards range up the slopes and ensure the tables of Garda's trattorias are stocked with fine wines and oils. Boats buzz across the water and songbirds fill the crumbling terraces of Sirmione's Roman ruins. All you need now is a vintage Alfa Romeo to tool around the lakeside admiring the views.

TRIP HIGHLIGHT

① Sirmione (p77)

Over the centuries impossibly pretty Sirmione has drawn the likes of Catullus and Maria Callas to its banks. The village sits astride a slender peninsula that juts out into the lake and is occupied in large part by the **Grotte di Catullo** (☏030 91 61 57; www. grottedicatullo.beniculturali.it; Piazzale Orti Manara 4; adult/reduced €6/3; ⏱8.30am-7.30pm Tue-Sat, 9.30am-6.30pm Sun Apr-Oct, 8.30am-2pm Tue-Sun Nov-Mar), a misnomer for the ruins of an extensive Roman villa now comprising teetering stone arches and tumbledown walls. There's no evidence that Catullus actually lived here, but who cares? The wraparound lake views from its terraced hillside are legendary.

In true Roman style, there's even an offshore thermal spring that pumps out water at a natural 37°C. Wallow lakeside in the outdoor pool at **Aquaria** (p77).

The Drive » The first 7km from Sirmione to Desenzano del Garda is on the SS572 lake road. Exit Sirmione past the Garda Village camp ground and at the first major roundabout turn right towards Desenzano.

② Desenzano del Garda

Known as the *porta del lago* (gateway to the lake), Desenzano may not be as pretty as other lakeside towns, but its ancient harbour, broad promenades and vibrant Piazza Matteotti make for pleasant wanderings. It is also a hub for summer nightlife.

Best of all are the mosaics in Desenzano's **Roman Villa** (☎030 914 35 47; Via Crocifisso 2; adult/reduced €2/1; ◷8.30am-7pm Mar-Oct, to 5pm Nov-Feb). Wooden walkways lead directly over vivid scenes of chariot-riding, grape-gathering cherubs.

Stretching north of Desenzano, the rolling hills of the Valtenesi are etched with vine trellises

LINK YOUR TRIP

3 Northern Cities
A 30-minute drive down the A22 and A4 brings you to Verona and the cultural Northern Cities tour (p37).

4 Roof of Italy
Climb out of the lake basin on the SS240 to Rovereto for a dose of modern art and an epic drive across Europe's highest pass (p45).

and olive groves, Garda's Mediterranean microclimate ensuring ideal olive-growing conditions. **Frantoio Montecroce** (www. frantoiomontecroce.it; Viale Ettore Andreis 84) offers tutored oil tastings.

The Drive » From Desenzano return to the SS572 and start to meander north right by the lake shore. The first 6km to Padenghe sul Garda are some of the most scenic on the lake, with cypresses and umbrella pines and clear views over the water.

TRIP HIGHLIGHT

❸ Salò (p77)

Sedate and refined as Salò is today, in 1943 it was named the capital of the Social Republic of Italy as part of Mussolini's last-ditch efforts to organise Italian fascism in the face of advancing Allied forces. This episode, known as the Republic of Salò, saw more than 16 buildings turned into Mussolini's ministries and offices. Strolling between the sites is a surreal tour. The tourist office has an English-language booklet featuring significant locations.

Offshore you may spot the small, comma-shaped **Isola del Garda** (☏328 6126943; www. isoladelgarda.com; tour incl boat ride €25-30; ☼Apr-Oct) crowned with neo-Gothic battlements and frothing with a luxuriant formal garden. It is the home of Contessa Cavazza and her family, who will host you on a two-hour guided tour of the villa's opulent rooms. Boats depart from Salò, Gardone Riviera, Garda and Sirmione.

The Drive » Exit the medieval centre of Salò uphill on Via Umberto I and pick up the SS45bis heading north to Gardone. It's barely 7km along the narrow single

carriageway, past old stone walls hiding lemon-coloured villas surrounded by luxuriant flora.

❹ Gardone Riviera (p78)

In Gardone tour the home of Italy's most controversial poet, Gabriele d'Annunzio. Poet, soldier, hypochondriac and proto-fascist, d'Annunzio's home **Il Vittoriale degli Italiani** (☏0365 29 65 11; www. vittoriale.it; Piazza Vittoriale; gardens & museums adult/ reduced €16/12; ☼grounds 8.30am-8pm Apr-Sep, to 5pm Oct-Mar, museums 8.30am-6.30pm Tue-Sun Apr-Sep, 9am-1pm & 2-5pm Tue-Sun Oct-Mar) is as bombastic and extravagant as it is unsettling, and the decor certainly sheds light on the man. He retreated to Gardone in 1922, claiming that he wanted to escape the world that made him sick.

For something less oppressive visit the flower-filled oasis of **Fondazione André Heller** (☏336 41 08 77; www.hellergarden.com; Via Roma 2; adult/child €10/5; ☼9am-7pm Mar-Oct), designed in the 1990s by multimedia artist André Heller. Hidden among the greenery are 30 pieces of contemporary sculpture.

The Drive » Exit Gardone northeast on Corso Zanardelli for a long, scenic 43km drive north. At Tignale and Limone

---

✓ TOP TIP: LAKE CRUISING

Fleets of ferries link many Lake Garda communities, providing a series of scenic mini-cruises. They're run by **Navigazione sul Lago di Garda** (www. navigazionelaghi.it), which publishes English-language timetables online. A one-day, unlimited travel ticket costs €25.80/13.40 per adult/child. A return fare for a single trip is €4.40.

Car ferries cross year-round from Toscolano-Maderno on the west bank to Torri del Benaco on the east bank.

Waterfront views at Sirmione (p30)

sul Garda you'll pass the stone pillars of Garda's lemon-houses. The final 12km from Limone to Riva del Garda are extraordinary, passing through dynamite-blasted tunnels dramatic enough to make this the location for the opening chase scene in *Casino Royale*.

- - - - - - - - - - -

TRIP HIGHLIGHT

⑤ Riva del Garda (p79)

Even on a lake blessed by dramatic scenery, Riva del Garda still comes out on top. Encircled by towering rock faces and a looping landscaped waterfront, its appealing centre is a medley of grand architecture and wide squares. The town's strategic position was fought over for centuries and exhibits in the **Museo Alto Garda** (p79) reflect this turbulent past.

Riva makes a natural starting point for walks and bike rides, including trails around **Monte Rocchetta** (1575m), which looms over the northern end of the lake. Immediately south of the town is the shingle beach and landscaped park, cut throughout with a cycle path that extends 3km to neighbouring **Torbole**.

The other natural spectacle worth a trip is the **Cascata del Varone** (www.cascata-varone.com; admission €5.50; ☉9am-7pm May-Aug, to 6pm Apr & Sep, to 5pm Mar & Oct), a 100m waterfall that thunders down the sheer limestone cliffs into a dripping gorge.

The Drive » From Riva pick up the SS240 around Torbole and then turn south on the SS249. Lake views abound through columned 'windows' as you pass through mountain tunnels, and to the left Monte Baldo rises above the lake. A cable car runs to the summit from Malcesine, from where it's 22km to Torri del Benaco.

water, while cypresses line front lawns to your left.

TRIP HIGHLIGHT

❻ Torri del Benaco

Picturesque Torri del Benaco is one of the most appealing stops on the eastern bank. The 14th-century **Castello Scaligero** (Viale Fratelli Lavanda 2; adult/reduced €3/1; ⏱9.30am-12.30pm & 2.30-6pm Apr–mid-Jun & mid-Sep–Oct, 9.30am-1pm & 4.30-7.30pm mid-Jun–mid-Sep) overlooks a pint-sized harbour and packs a wealth of history into dozens of rooms, including exhibits on the lake's traditional industries of fishing, olive-oil production and lemon growing.

The Drive ≫ From the waterfront at Torri del Benaco it's a short 7km drive to Garda, around the headland. En route low stone walls or railings are all that stand between you and the

❼ Garda

The bustling town of Garda lacks obvious charms, but it does boast the leafy headland of **Punta San Vigilio**, a gorgeous crescent bay backed by olive trees 3km to the north. The privately owned **Parco Baia delle Sirene** (www.parcobaiadellesirene; Punta San Vigilio; ⏱10am-7pm Apr-May, to 8pm Jun-Sep; 👫) has sun loungers and picnic tables beneath the trees; there's also a children's play area. Prices are seasonal and range from €5 to €12 per adult (€2 to €5 per child) per day.

The tiny headland is also the location of **Locanda San Vigilio** (☎045 725 41 90; www.locanda-sanvigilio.it; Punta San

Vigilio; buffet €45; ⏱10am-5.30pm), with its excellent harbourside taverna. Book for one of the truly memorable candlelight buffets on Friday and Saturday.

The Drive ≫ The final 5km drive to Bardolino, continuing on the SS249, gives you your final fill of big views. Over the short distance the road rises up, giving you lofty views over the water before dropping down amid olive groves into Bardolino.

DETOUR:
LAGO DI LEDRO

Start: ❺ **Riva del Garda**

From Riva take the SP37 and then the SS240 west into the mountains, past olive groves and vine-lined terraces. After 11km the road flattens and **Lago di Ledro** (www.vallediledro.com) comes into view. Only 2.5km long and 2km wide, this diminutive lake sits at an altitude of 650m and is set in a gorgeous valley beneath tree-covered mountains. **Molina di Ledro** is at the lake's eastern end, where thatched huts line up beside beaches and boat-hire pontoons.

Bardolino vineyards overlooking Lake Garda

❽ Bardolino (p80)

More than 70 vineyards and wine cellars grace the gentle hills that roll east from Bardolino's shores, many within DOC and the even stricter DOCG regional quality-control classifications. They produce an impressive array of pink Chiaretto, ruby Classico, dry Superiore and young Novello.

One of the most atmospheric ways to savour their flavours is a tutored tasting at **Guerrieri Rizzardi** (☎045 721 00 28; www. guerrieri-rizzardi.com; Via Verdi 4; tastings €15; ⏱5pm Wed May-Oct). After a tour of the wine cellars, tastings take place in the kitchen garden, with tables laid out beside an orangery and a vineyard labyrinth.

Bardolino is at its most Bacchic during the **Festa dell'Uva e del Vino** in early October, when the town's waterfront fills with food and wine stands.

Northern Cities

3

The Po valley, with its waving fields of corn and rice paddies, hosts some of Italy's most handsome and prosperous towns, from Milan and Bergamo in the west to Verona and Venice in the east.

TRIP HIGHLIGHTS

375 km

Venice
Explore the drama and intrigue of the Palazzo Ducale

257 km

Verona
Shout 'Brava!' for opera diva encores at the Arena

Bergamo ●

Milan
START

Vicenza
●

Mestre

6

Soave

7

8

FINISH

5

219 km

Mantua
Renowned for Mantegna's frescoes and fine dining

334 km

Padua
See the Renaissance dawning in Giotto's moving frescoes

7–10 DAYS
375KM / 233 MILES

GREAT FOR...

BEST TIME TO GO
September to May to avoid the crowds.

ESSENTIAL PHOTO
The golden domes and precious mosaics of San Marco in Venice.

BEST FOR SURPRISES
The little-known treasures in Bergamo's Accademia Carrara.

3 Northern Cities

Ever since Julius Caesar granted Roman citizenship to the people of the plains, the Po valley has prospered. Wend your way through the cornfields from the Lombard powerhouse of Milan to Roman Brixia (Brescia), the Gonzaga stronghold of Mantua and the serene Republic of Venice. This is a land of legends spun by Virgil, Dante and Shakespeare, where grand dynasties fought for power and patronised some of the finest works of art in the world.

❶ Milan (p54)

From Charlemagne to Napoleon, and even Silvio Berlusconi, mercantile Milan (Milano) has always attracted the moneyed and the Machiavellian. Follow the city's changing fortunes through the frescoed halls of the **Castello Sforzesco** (📞02 8846 3703; www.milanocastello .it; Piazza Castello; adult/ reduced €5/3; ⏱9am-7.30pm Tue-Sun, to 10.30pm Thu; Ⓜ Cairoli), some of them decorated by

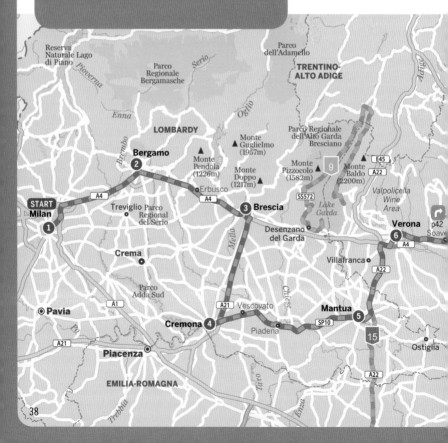

Leonardo da Vinci, where exquisite sculptures, paintings and weapons tell the turbulent tale of the city. From its ramparts, look out over the **Parco Sempione** and spy the pearly pinnacles of the **Duomo** (www. duomomilano.it; Piazza del Duomo; roof terraces adult/ reduced via stairs €8/4, lift €13/7, Battistero di San Giovanni €4/2; ⊙duomo 7am-6.40pm, roof terraces 9am-6.30pm, battistero 10am-6pm Tue-Sun; [M]Duomo) . Begun in 1387 it took six centuries to build, rushed to completion in the 19th

century so that Napoleon could crown himself King of Italy in its cavernous interior.

True to Milan's spirit of free enterprise, one of the city's finest art collections is the private collection of **Museo Poldi-Pezzoli** (www.museopoldipezzoli.it; Via Alessandro Manzoni 12; adult/ reduced €9/6; ⊙10am-6pm Wed-Mon), where priceless Bellinis and Botticellis hang in Pezzoli's 19th-century *palazzo* (mansion). From here it's a few steps to the city's 'Golden Quadrangle' of designer shops.

The Drive ⟩⟩ Make your way northeast out of town along Corso Venezia, or via the A52 ring road, depending on where you're staying in town. Merge with the A4 Milan–Brescia autostrada for an uneventful 56km drive to Bergamo.

- - - - - - - - - -

❷ Bergamo (p81)

Beautiful Bergamo, its domes and towers piled on a promontory at the foot of the Alps, is one of the most arresting urban views in Italy. Le Corbusier found its **Piazza Vecchia** 'the most beautiful square in Europe', the magnificent ensemble of medieval and Renaissance buildings much influenced by Venetian fashions, with the lion of St Mark's emblazoned on the **Palazzo della Ragione**. The latter currently hosts works from the **Accademia Carrara** (p83), one of Italy's great art repositories.

Through the arches of the Palazzo della Ragione you'll glimpse

🔗 LINK YOUR TRIP

2 **A Weekend at Lake Garda**

Got an urge for the outdoors? Jump off the A4 before Verona to Desenzano del Garda and mess around Lake Garda for a weekend (p29).

a second square, the **Piazza Duomo**, fronted by the extraordinary polychromatic marble facade of the **Cappella Colleoni** (⊙9am-12.30pm & 2-4.30pm Tue-Sun Nov-Feb, 9am-12.30pm & 2-6.30pm Mar-Oct), the mausoleum-cum-chapel of Venice's most famous mercenary commander, Bartolomeo Colleoni (1696–1770).

The Drive ≫ Leave Bergamo via the *citta bassa* (lower town) southwards and rejoin the A4 in the direction of Brescia. Surprisingly, this 55km stretch is relatively scenic, especially as you drive through the wine region of Franciacorta.

- - - - - - - - - -

❸ Brescia (p84)

Despite its seedy urban periphery, Brescia's old town contains some of the most important Roman ruins in Lombardy and an extraordinary, circular Roman church, the **Duomo Vecchio** (Piazza Paolo VI; ⊙9am-noon & 3-6pm Wed-Sat, 9-10.45am & 3-6pm Sun), built over the ancient Roman baths.

From here the Via dei Musei, the ancient *decumanus maximus* (east–west main street), leads to the heart of Roman Brixia, **Piazza del Foro**, which sits beneath the columns of the **Tempio Capitolino**, erected by Vespasian in AD 73 and preserved for posterity by a medieval mudslide. Next to the

ruined temple is the unexcavated *cavea* (semicircular, tiered auditorium) of the **Teatro Romano** (p84), and beside that the **Monastero di Santa Giulia** (Museo della Città; ☎030 297 78 34; www.brescia musei.com; Via dei Musei 81; adult/reduced €10/5.50; ⊙10.30am-7pm Tue-Sun mid-Jun–Sep, shorter hours winter), a vast monastery complex and museum that charts the layers of Brescian history. Best of all are the two Roman houses, which were absorbed wholesale into the monastery. Their mosaic floors and frescoes are real highlights.

The Drive ≫ Wend your way southwards out of Brescia's complicated suburbs following signs for the A21. Smaller and less heavily trafficked than the A4, the 53km drive to Cremona takes you through some unspoilt farmland dotted with the occasional farmhouse.

- - - - - - - - - -

❹ Cremona (p88)

Famous for violins, nougat and the tallest bell tower in Italy (111m), Cremona is a charming stopover. The stout-hearted can climb the 502 steps to the top of the *campanile* for scenic views. The **cathedral** (Piazza del Comune; ⊙8am-noon & 2.30-6pm Mon-Sat, noon-12.30pm & 3.30-6pm Sun) next door is one of the most exuberant expressions of

Lombard Romanesque architecture.

Aside from the views, Cremona made a name for itself as the violin capital of Europe, after Andrea Amati discovered in 1566 that with a bit of adjustment his old medieval fiddle could be made to sing the sweetest tunes. By the 18th century Andrea's son, Nicolò Amati, his pupil Antonio Stradivarius and Giuseppe Guarneri were crafting the best violins ever. See the originals in climate-controlled cases in the **Collezione Gli Archi di Palazzo Comunale** (http:// musei.comune.cremona.it; Piazza del Comune 8; adult/ reduced €6/4; ⊙9am-6pm Tue-Sat, 10am-6pm Sun). Afterwards visit the **Museo Civico** (Via Ugolani Dati 4; adult/reduced €7/5; ⊙9am-6pm Tue-Sat, 10am-6pm Sun) to see how they are crafted.

The Drive ≫ You're off the main roads between Cremona and Mantua. Take Via Mantova east out of town and join the SP10. The tree-lined single carriageway passes through cornfields and the small towns of Vescovato and Piadena before reaching the watery outskirts of Mantua.

- - - - - - - - - -

TRIP HIGHLIGHT

❺ Mantua (p85)

The Latin poet Virgil was born just outside Mantua (Mantova) in 70 BC, and the modern town

Piazza delle Erbe, Verona

preserves its antique timeline in its art and architecture. Ruled by the Gonzaga dynasty for three centuries, the court attracted artists of the highest calibre, including Pisanello, Rubens and, more famously, Andrea Mantegna, who was court painter from 1460 until his death in 1506. It's their dazzling frescoes that decorate the **Palazzo Ducale** ([☎]041 241 18 97; www.ducalemantova.org; Piazza Sordello 40; adult/reduced €13/8; [🕑]8.15am-7.15pm Tue-Sun). During busy periods you may have to book to see the biggest draw – Mantegna's 15th-century frescoes in the **Camera degli Sposi** (Bridal Chamber).

Hardly more modest in scale is the Gonzaga's suburban villa, the **Palazzo Te** (www.palazzote.it; Viale Te; adult/reduced €8/5; [🕑]1-6pm Mon, 9am-6pm Tue-Sun). Mainly used by Duke Federico II as a place of rendezvous with his mistress, Isabella Boschetti, it is decorated in playboy style with playful motifs and encoded love symbols.

The Drive » From Mantua head almost directly north for Verona. Leave town on Via Legnago, crossing the causeway that separates Lago di Mezzo from Lago Inferiore, then pick up the A22 autostrada for an easy 30km drive to Verona.

- - - - - - - - - - - -

TRIP HIGHLIGHT

6 Verona

Shakespeare placed star-crossed Romeo Montague and Juliet Capulet in Verona for good reason: romance, drama and fatal family feuds have been the city's hallmark for centuries.

From the 3rd century BC, Verona was a Roman trade centre, with ancient gates, a forum (now Piazza delle Erbe) and a grand **Roman Arena** (www.arena.it; Piazza Brà; free with Verona Card, adult/reduced €6/4.50; [🕑]1.30-7.30pm Mon, 8.30am-7.30pm Tue-Sun), which still hosts live summer opera performances. But Shakespearean tragedy came with the territory.

After Mastino della Scala (aka Scaligeri) lost re-election to Verona's commune in 1262, he claimed absolute control, until murdered by his rivals. On the north side of **Piazza dei Signori** stands the early-Renaissance **Loggia del Consiglio**, the 15th-century city council. Through the archway you'll find the **Arche Scaligere** – elaborate Gothic tombs of the Scaligeri family, where murderers are interred

41

next to the relatives they killed.

Paranoid for good reason, the fratricidal Cangrande II (1351–59) built the **Castelvecchio** (📞045 806 26 11; Corso Castelvecchio 2; free with Verona Card, adult/reduced €6/4.50; ⏱1.30-7.30pm Mon, 8.30am-7.30pm Tue-Sun) to guard the river Adige, which snakes through town. Now it houses Verona's main museum with works by Tiepolo, Carpaccio and Veronese.

For discounted entry to all of Verona's major monuments, museums and churches, plus unlimited travel on city buses, consider purchasing a Verona Card (two/five days €15/20), on sale at most major tourist sights as well as tobacconists.

The Drive » The 90km drive from Verona to Padua is once again along the A4. This stretch of road is heavily trafficked by heavy-goods vehicles. The only rewards are glimpses of Soave's crenulated castle to your left and the tall church spire of Monteforte d'Alpone. You could also extend your trip with a stop to take in the World Heritage architecture of Vicenza.

- - - - - - - - - -

TRIP HIGHLIGHT

⑦ Padua (p100)

Dante, da Vinci, Boccaccio and Vasari all honour Giotto as the artist who officially ended the Dark Ages. Giotto's startlingly humanist approach not only changed how people saw the heavenly company, it changed how they saw themselves; not as lowly vassals but as vessels for the divine, however flawed. This humanising approach was especially well suited to the **Cappella degli Scrovegni** (Scrovegni Chapel; www. cappelladegliscrovegni.it; Piazza Eremitani 8; adult/ reduced €13/6, night ticket €8/6; ⏱9am-7pm, also 7-10pm various periods through year), the chapel in Padua (Padova) that Enrico Scrovegni commissioned in memory of his father, who as a moneylender was denied a Christian burial. Think how radical the scenes must have been for medieval churchgoers witnessing familiar situations such as exhausted new dad Joseph asleep in the manger or onlookers gossiping as middle-aged Anne tenderly kisses Joachim.

Afterwards, tour the **Musei Civici agli Eremitani** (📞049 820 45 51; Piazza Eremitani 8; adult/ reduced €10/8; ⏱ 9am-7pm Tue-Sun) for pre-Roman Padua downstairs and a pantheon of Veneto artists upstairs.

The Drive » The 40km drive from Padua to Venice is through a tangle of suburban neighbourhoods and featureless areas of light industry along the A4 and then the A57.

DETOUR: SOAVE

Start: ⑥ Verona

East of Verona, Soave serves its namesake DOC white wine in a storybook setting. Built by Verona's fratricidal Scaligeri family, the **Castello di Soave** encompasses an early Renaissance villa, grassy courtyards and the **Mastio** – a defensive tower apparently used as a dungeon. More inviting is the **Azienda Agricola Coffele** (📞045 768 00 07; www.coffele. it; Via Roma 5; ⏱9am-12.30pm & 2-7pm Mon-Sat), a family-run winery across from the church in the old town, where you can taste the lemon-zesty DOC Soave Classico and the bubbly DOCG Recioto di Soave, both bearing the regional quality-control standard of the Denominazione di Origine Controllata (DOC).

TRIP HIGHLIGHT

8 Venice (p90)

Like its signature landmark, the **Basilica di San Marco** (www. basilicasanmarco.it; Piazza San Marco; basilica entry free; ⏰9.45am-5pm Mon-Sat, 2-5pm Sun summer, to 4pm Sun winter; 🚤San Marco), the Venetian empire was dazzlingly cosmopolitan. Armenians, Turks, Greeks and Germans were neighbours along the **Grand Canal**, and Jewish communities persecuted elsewhere in Europe founded publishing houses and banks. By the mid-15th century, Venice (Venezia) was swathed in golden mosaics, imported silks and clouds of incense.

Don't be fooled though by the Gothic elegance: underneath the lacy pink cladding the **Palazzo Ducale** (Ducal Palace; www. palazzoducale.visitmuve.it; Piazzetta San Marco 52; adult/ reduced incl Museo Correr €18/11; ⏰8.30am-7pm summer, to 5.30pm winter; 🚤San Zaccaria) ran an uncompromising dictatorship. Discover state secrets on the **Itinerari Segreti** (📞041 4273 0892; adult/reduced €18/12; ⏰tours in English 9.55am, 10.45am & 11.35am), which takes you to the

THE ORIGINAL GHETTO

In medieval times, the Cannaregio outpost in Venice housed a *getto* (foundry) – but as the designated Jewish quarter from the 16th to 18th centuries, this area gave the word a whole new meaning. In accordance with the Venetian Republic's 1516 decree, Jewish lenders, doctors and clothing merchants were allowed to attend to Venice's commercial interests by day, while at night and on Christian holidays most were restricted to the gated island of **Ghetto Nuovo**.

When Jewish merchants fled the Spanish Inquisition for Venice in 1541, there was no place to go in the Ghetto but up: around **Campo del Ghetto Nuovo**, upper storeys housed new arrivals. Despite a 10-year censorship order issued by the church in Rome in 1553, Jewish Venetian publishers contributed hundreds of titles popularising new Renaissance ideas on religion, humanist philosophy and medicine.

sinister Trial Chamber and Interrogation Room.

Centuries later, Napoleon took some of Venice's finest heirlooms to France. But the biggest treasure in the **Museo Correr** (www. museiciviciveneziani.it; Piazza San Marco 52; ⏰10am-7pm Apr-Oct, to 5pm Nov-Mar) couldn't be lifted: Jacopo Sansovino's **Libreria Nazionale Marciana**, covered with larger-than-life philosophers by Veronese, Titian and Tintoretto.

For more visual commentary on Venetian high life, head for the **Gallerie dell'Accademia** (www.gallerieaccademia.org; Campo della Carità 1050; adult/ reduced €11/8 plus supplement during special exhibitions, first Sun of the month free; ⏰8.15am-2pm Mon, to 7.15pm Tue-Sun; 🚤Accademia), whose hallowed halls contain more murderous intrigue and forbidden romance than most Venetian parties.

You cannot take your car onto the lagoon islands so leave it in a secure garage in Mestre, such as **Garage Europa** (www.garageeuropamestre. com; per day €14), and hop on the train to Venice Santa Lucia, where water taxis connect to all the islands.

Roof of Italy

4

Traversing the Alps, from Lake Como through the Valtellina's vine-covered slopes and across the hair-raising Passo dello Stelvio to Merano, this is one of the north's most spectacular roads.

TRIP HIGHLIGHTS

192 km

Merano
Float away beneath palm trees and snowy peaks

116 km

Bormio
Roman spring and gateway to the Stelvio's 'Magnifica Terra'

● Trafoi
③

Caldaro ●

④

Tirano
②

Alto Lario ●
START

⑦ **FINISH**

The Valtellina
Alpine foothills covered in steeply terraced vineyards

69 km

Rovereto
Discover a world-class contemporary art collection

290 km

6 DAYS
290KM / 180 MILES

GREAT FOR...

BEST TIME TO GO
June to September, when the Passo dello Stelvio is open.

ESSENTIAL PHOTO
Cloud-busting views on the Passo dello Stelvio.

BEST FOR WELL-BEING
Dipping in Merano's hot and cold spa pools amid mountain peaks.

Left Passo dello Stelvio (p48)

4 Roof of Italy

Tracing the foothills of the Orobie Alps and the high passes of Parco Nazionale dello Stelvio, the borderlands of northern Italy offer up stunning wildernesses, stupendous scenery and warm welcomes in wooden farmhouses. Vineyards and orchards cloak the valleys of the Valtellina and Adige, while the region's historic cities – Merano, Trento and Rovereto – combine Austrian and Italian influences, creating a unique cultural and culinary melange.

❶ Alto Lario

The towns of **Dongo**, **Gravedona** and **Sorico** once formed the independent republic of the Tre Pievi (Three Parishes) and were a hotbed of Cathar heresy. Now they're more popular with water-sports enthusiasts than Inquisitors. Lake Lario is another name for Lake Como (Lago di Como), so the area takes its name from being at the top *(alto)*

p49

of the lake. Gravedona, the largest of the three towns, sits on a gently curved bay with views across to Monte Legnone.

Up on the plateau at Peglio, **Chiesa di Sant'Eusebio** (⏱3-6pm Thu, Sat & Sun Jul-Sep) offers lake views and masterly frescoes by Como painter Giovan Mauro della Rovere, better known as Il Fiammenghino (Little Fleming). He sought refuge here after murdering a man and did penance painting the vivid *Last Judgement*.

Sorico, the most northerly of the three towns, guards the mouth of the river Mera, which flows into shallow **Lago di Mezzola**, once part of Lake Como and now a bird-breeding nature reserve.

The Drive » From Sorico take the SS340dir north. Cross over the waterway that connects Lake Como and Lago di Mezzola and continue until you hit a T-junction. Turn right, and at the roundabout turn left onto the SS38 towards Morbengo. Continue for a further 26km, chasing the Adda river all the way to Sondrio.

TRIP HIGHLIGHT

❷ The Valtellina (p113)

The Valtellina cuts a broad swath down the Adda valley, where villages and vineyards hang precariously on the slopes of the Orobie Alps. The steep northern flank is carpeted by Nebbiolo grapes, which yield a light-red wine. Both body and alcohol content improve with altitude, so generations of Valtenesi built upwards, carrying the soil in woven baskets to high mountain terraces. Their rewards: a DOC regional quality-standard classification for Valtellina Superiore since 1968. In **Sondrio**, it's possible to visit the cellars of **Pellizzatti Perego** (www.arpepe.com; Via Buon Consiglio 4), and in **Chiuri**, **Nino Negri** (www.ninonegri.it; Via Ghibellini 3).

The prettiest town in the valley is **Tirano**, where mule trains once came from Venice and

LINK YOUR TRIP

1 The Graceful Italian Lakes

Take the scenic SS340dir to Tremezzo to tour Como's luxuriant gardens and Maggiore's Borromean palaces. (p17)

TOP TIP:
PASSO DELLO STELVIO

The high and hair-raising Passo dello Stelvio is only open from June to September, and is always subject to closures dependent on early or late snow falls. For the rest of the year, Bormio is best approached from Sondalo in Lombardy, or via Tubre into Switzerland to take the Munt la Schera tunnel to Livigno.

Brescia, and which is now the departure point for the **Trenino Rosso del Bernina** (☎342 70 62 63; www.treninorosso.it; one-way/ return €24.50/49), a gravity-defying rail track that traverses 196 bridges, crests the Bernina Pass (2253m) and crosses the Morteratsch glacier on the way to St Moritz in Switzerland.

The Drive >> From Tirano it is 37 scenic kilometres to the heady heights of Bormio. Continue northeast on the SS38, still tracking the Adda river and rising up through the terraces, past small hamlets such as Grosio and Sondalo and into the snow-capped mountains.

- - - - - - - - - -

TRIP HIGHLIGHT

③ Bormio

Splendidly sited in a mountain basin at 1225m, Bormio was once the heart of a region dubbed Magnifica Terra. Most of the region's magnificent territory now lies within northern Italy's largest national park, the **Parco Nazionale dello Stelvio** (www.parks.it/parco.nazionale. stelvio), an icy land of 100

glaciers that includes one of Europe's largest, the **Ghiacciaio dei Forni**.

The Stelvio is largely the preserve of walkers, who come for the extensive network of well-organised mountain huts and marked trails – but there are a couple of well-serviced ski runs at **Solda** and the **Passo dello Stelvio** (2757m), both of which offer year-round skiing.

Back in Bormio's medieval centre, the **Bagni di Bormio** (www. bagnidibormio.it; Via Statale Stelvio; spa passes €41-45; ⏰10am-8pm, New Baths to 11pm Fri & Sat) was much loved by the likes of Pliny the Elder and Leonardo da Vinci. Hotel stays include unlimited spa access, but day passes are also available.

The Drive >> The most difficult, and awe-inspiring, 96km is the spectacular road from Bormio to Merano, which crosses the cloud-covered Stelvio pass, 25km from Bormio. Approaching along the SS38, the road rises through a series of tight switchbacks, some with very steep gradients, and descends via equally alarming

hairpin bends to quaint Trafoi on the other side. One of the highest roads in Europe, it is not for the faint-hearted. From Trafoi continue on the SS38 all the way to Merano.

- - - - - - - - - -

TRIP HIGHLIGHT

④ Merano (p110)

Merano is where 19th-century Mitteleuropeans came to soothe their weary bones, do a 'grape' cure, and, perhaps, embark on a dalliance or two. The Hapsburg-era spa was the hot destination of its day and the city's therapeutic traditions have served it well in the new millennium, with the striking modern redevelopment of the **Terme Merano** (☎0473 25 20 00; www.thermemeran. it; Piazza Terme 1; bathing pass 2hr/all day €12.50/18; ⏰9am-10pm). Swim through the sluice towards 12 outdoor pools in summer and be met by a vision of palm-studded gardens and snow-topped mountains beyond.

You could also give over an entire day to the botanical gardens at **Castel Trauttmansdorff** (www.trauttmansdorff.it; Via San Valentino 51a; garden & museum adult/reduced €12/10; ⏰9am-6pm Apr-Nov, to 11pm Fri summer), where exotic cacti and palms, beds of lilies, irises and tulips all cascade down the hillside surrounding a castle where Sissi

Terme Merano

(Empress Elisabeth) spent the summer.

The Drive » From Merano to Bolzano and the Castello Firmiano, the SS38 becomes a dual-lane autostrada, so the next 29km are easy motorway driving as you leave the high mountains behind you.

- - - - - - - - - - -

⑤ Castel Firmiano (p108)

Known as the 'Crown of Sigismund', the expansive walls and battlements of Castel Firmiano encircle the hilltop overlooking Bolzano and Appiano just like a princely coronet. Fought over for 1000 years, it has long been

a symbol of Tyrolean independence and now houses the **Messner Mountain Museum**

(☎0471 63 31 45; www.messner-mountain-museum.it; Via Castel Firmiano 53; adult/reduced €10/8; ☺10am-6pm

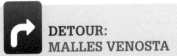

DETOUR: MALLES VENOSTA

Start: ③ Bormio

Just north of Bormio on the scenic SS40 sits the old customs point of Malles Venosta. Aside from its handsome Gothic churches and historic centre, it sits just beneath the vast **Abbazia di Monte Maria** (☎0473 84 39 80; www.marienberg.it; Schlinig 1, Malles; admission €5; ☺10am-4pm Mon-Sat), the highest Benedictine monastery in Europe. In the crypt are a series of superb Byzantine-Romanesque frescoes, which were only discovered in 1980. Their almost pristine condition makes them quite unique.

Fri-Wed Mar-Nov), named after celebrated mountaineer Reinhold Messner. Exhibits explore humanity's relationship with the mountains while the inspiring design, involving hundreds of stairs, suggests shifting altitudes and uneven mountain terrain.

South of the castle stretches the **Weinstrasse** (see p112), a wine road winding through the Adige valley along the SP14 all the way to Trento. Producers line the route although the hub of the region is **Caldaro**.

The Drive » South of Bolzano the autostrada carves a straight line through the midst of the Adige valley. It's a fast, scenic route with the mountains overlapping in descending order in front of you. If you have more time, however, the preferred route is to pick up the SP14 from the castle to Caldaro and follow the wine route all the way to Magré, where you can stop and taste some of the prized Adige wines.

- - - - - - - - - - -

⑥ Trento (p104)

During the tumultuous years of the Counter-Reformation, the Council of Trent convened here, dishing out far-reaching condemnations to uppity Protestants. Modern Trento is less preachy: quietly confident and easy to like. Frescoed streets fan out from

the **Duomo** (⏰6.30am-6pm), which sits above a 6th-century temple and a **Paleo-Christian archaeological area** (adult/reduced incl with nearby Museo Diocesano €5/3; ⏰10am-noon & 2.30-5.30pm Mon-Sat).

On the opposite side of the square is the former bishop's residence, **Palazzo Pretoria** (☎0461 23 44 19; Piazza del Duomo 18; adult/reduced €4/2.50; ⏰9.30am-12.30pm & 2.30-6pm Wed-Mon), where illuminated manuscripts and paintings depict the Council of Trent.

Above it all, the mighty **Castello del Buonconsiglio** (☎0461 23 37 70; www.buonconsiglio. it; Via Clesio 5; adult/reduced €8/5; ⏰9.30am-5pm Tue-Sun) is a reminder of the bloody history of these borderlands. During WWI, Italian patriot Cesare Battisti was held in the castle dungeon before being hanged by the Austrians as a traitor.

The Drive » The final 30km drive south on the A22 leaves most of the majestic scenery behind, and the broad valley tapers out towards Rovereto.

- - - - - - - - - - -

TRIP HIGHLIGHT

⑦ Rovereto (p107)

In the winter of 1769, Leopold Mozart and his soon-to-be-famous musical son visited Rovereto. Those on a musical pilgrimage come

to visit the **Church of San Marco** (Piazza St Marco; ⏰8.30am-noon & 2-7pm), where the 13-year-old Wolfgang wowed the Roveretini, and for the annual **Mozart Festival** (www.festivalmozartrovereto. com) in August.

The town that Mozart knew still has its tightly coiled streets, but it's the shock of the new that lures most to the **Museo di Arte Moderna e Contemporanea** (MART; ☎0464 43 88 87; english.mart.trento. it; Corso Bettini 43; adult/reduced €11/7, incl Casa del Depero €13/9; ⏰10am-6pm Tue-Thu, Sat & Sun, to 9pm Fri), one of Italy's best 20th-century art museums. Designed by Ticinese architect Mario Botta, it is a fitting home for some huge 20th-century works, including Warhol's *Four Marilyns* (1962), several Picassos and a clutch of contemporary art stars. Italian work is, naturally, well represented, with excellent pieces from Balla, Morandi, de Chirico, Fontana and Manzoni.

Fishing in the Adige River, Rovereto

51

Destinations

Milan (p54)

Home to the nation's stock exchange, one of Europe's biggest trade-fair grounds and an international fashion hub, Milan is also Italy's economic powerhouse.

Around Milan (p66)

Beyond Milan pretty countryside unfolds, while to the north a burst of Mediterranean colour and a balmy microclimate await around the lakes.

Venice & Padua (p90)

A fabled lagoon city awash with art, music and spice-route cuisine, and a medieval city-state home to Italy's second-oldest university.

Trento & the North (p104)

The provinces of Trentino and Alto Adige offer up a number of stunning wilderness areas, where adventure and comfort can be found in equal measure.

Galleria Vittorio Emanuele mall, Milan
CULTURA RM EXCLUSIVE/ANTHONY CHARLES/GETTY IMAGES ©

At Lombardy's heart is Milan, capital of the north and Italy's second-largest metropolis. Home to the nation's stock exchange, one of Europe's biggest trade-fair grounds and an international fashion hub, it is also Italy's economic powerhouse.

Milan

MILAN

POP 1.3 MILLION

Milan is Italy's city of the future, a fast-paced metropolis with New World qualities: ambition, aspiration and a highly individualistic streak. In Milan appearances really do matter and materialism requires no apology. The Milanese love beautiful and luxurious things, and it is for that reason perhaps that Italian fashion and design maintain their esteemed global position.

But like the models that work the catwalks, Milan is considered by many to be vain, distant and dull. And it is true that the city makes little effort to seduce visitors. However, this superficial lack of charm disguises a city of ancient roots and many treasures, which, unlike in the rest of Italy, you'll often get to experience without the queues. So while the Milanese may not always play nice, jump in and join them regardless in their intoxicating round of pursuits, whether that means precision-shopping, browsing edgy contemporary galleries or loading up a plate with local delicacies while downing an expertly mixed negroni cocktail.

◉ Sights

Milan's runway-flat terrain and monumental buildings are defined by concentric ring roads that trace the path of the city's original defensive walls. Although very little remains of the walls, ancient *porta* (gates) act as clear compass points. Almost everything you want to see, do or buy is contained within these city gates.

★ Duomo
CATHEDRAL

(Map p62; www.duomomilano.it; Piazza del Duomo; roof terraces adult/reduced via stairs €8/4, lift €13/7, Battistero di San Giovanni €4/2; ⊙duomo 7am-6.40pm, roof terraces 9am-6.30pm, battistero 10am-6pm Tue-Sun; Ⓜ Duomo) A vision in pink Candoglia marble, Milan's extravagant Gothic cathedral, 600 years in the making, aptly reflects the city's creativity and ambition. Its pearly white facade, adorned with 135 spires and 3400 statues, rises like the filigree of a fairy-tale tiara, wowing the crowds with its extravagant detail. The interior is no less impressive, punctuated by the largest stained-glass windows in Christendom, while in the crypt saintly Carlo Borromeo is interred in a rock-crystal casket.

Palazzo Reale
MUSEUM, PALACE

(Map p62; ✆02 87 56 72; www.comune.milano.it/palazzoreale; Piazza del Duomo 12; admission varies; ⊙exhibitions 2.30-7.30pm Mon, 9.30am-7.30pm Tue, Wed, Fri & Sun, to 10.30pm Thu & Sat; Ⓜ Duomo) Empress Maria Theresa's favourite architect, Giuseppe Piermarini, gave this town hall and Visconti palace a neoclassical overhaul in the late 18th century. The supremely elegant interiors were all but destroyed by WWII bombs; the Sala delle Cariatidi remains unrenovated as a reminder of war's indiscriminate destruction. Now the once-opulent palace hosts blockbuster art exhibits attracting serious crowds to shows as diverse as Warhol, Chagall, da Vinci and Giotto.

★ Museo del Novecento   GALLERY
(Map p62; ☏ 02 8844 4061; www.museodel novecento.org; Via Marconi 1; adult/reduced €5/3; ⊙ 2.30-7.30pm Mon, 9.30am-7.30pm Tue, Wed, Fri & Sun, to 10.30pm Thu & Sat; Ⓜ Duomo) Overlooking Piazza del Duomo, with fabulous views of the cathedral, is Mussolini's Arengario, from where he would harangue huge crowds in his heyday. Now it houses Milan's museum of 20th-century art. Built around a futuristic spiral ramp (an ode to the Guggenheim), the lower floors are cramped, but the heady collection, which includes the likes of Umberto Boccioni, Campigli, de Chirico and Marinetti, more than distracts.

Gallerie d'Italia   MUSEUM
(Map p62; www.gallerieditalia.com; Piazza della Scala 6; adult/reduced €10/8; ⊙ 9.30am-7.30pm Tue-Sun; Ⓜ Duomo) Housed in three fabulously decorated palaces, the enormous art collection of Fondazione Cariplo and Intesa Sanpaolo bank pays homage to 18th- and 19th-century Lombard painting. From a magnificent sequence of bas-reliefs by Antonio Canova to luminous Romantic masterpieces by Francesco Hayez, the works span 23 rooms and document Milan's significant contribution to the rebirth of Italian sculpture, the patriotic romanticism of the Risorgimento (reunification period) and the birth of futurism at the dawn of the 20th century.

★ Pinacoteca di Brera   GALLERY
(Map p62; ☏ 02 7226 3264; www.brera.beni culturali.it; Via Brera 28; adult/reduced €10/7; ⊙ 8.30am-7.15pm Tue-Sun; Ⓜ Lanza, Montenapoleone) Located upstairs from the centuries-old Accademia di Belle Arti (still one of Italy's most prestigious art schools), this gallery houses Milan's impressive collection of Old Masters, much of it 'lifted' from Venice by Napoleon. Rembrandt, Goya and Van Dyck all have a place in the collection, but look for the Italians: Titian, Tintoretto, Veronese, and the Bellini brothers. Much of the work has tremendous emotional clout, most notably Mantegna's brutal *Lamentation over the Dead Christ*.

Museo Poldi Pezzoli   MUSEUM
See p39.

Castello Sforzesco   CASTLE, MUSEUM
See p38.

Triennale di Milano   MUSEUM
(Map p56; ☏ 02 72 43 41; www.triennaledesign museum.it; Viale Emilio Alemanga 6; adult/reduced €8/6.50; ⊙ 10.30am-8.30pm Tue, Wed, Sat & Sun, to 11pm Thu & Fri; Ⓜ Cadorna) Italy's first Triennale took place in 1923 in Monza. It aimed to promote interest in Italian design and applied arts, from 'the spoon to the city', and its success led to the creation of Giovanni Muzio's Palazzo d'Arte in Milan in 1933. Since then this exhibition space has championed design in all its forms, although the triennale formula has since been replaced by long annual events, with international exhibits as part of the program.

★ The Last Supper   ARTWORK
(Il Cenacolo; Map p56; ☏ 02 9280 0360; www. cenacolovinciano.net; Piazza Santa Maria delle Grazie 2; adult/reduced €8/4.75; ⊙ 8.15am-7pm Tue-Sun; Ⓜ Cadorna) Milan's most famous mural, Leonardo da Vinci's *The Last Supper* (Il Cenacolo) is hidden away on a wall of the refectory adjoining the Basilica di Santa Maria delle Grazie (Map p56; www.grazieop. it; Piazza Santa Maria delle Grazie; ⊙ 7am-noon & 3-7.30pm Mon-Sat, 7.30am-12.30pm & 3.30-9pm Sun; Ⓜ Cadorna, 🚎16). Depicting Christ and his disciples at the dramatic moment when Christ reveals he's aware of his betrayal, it's

Interior of the Duomo di Milano (Milan Cathedral)

Milan

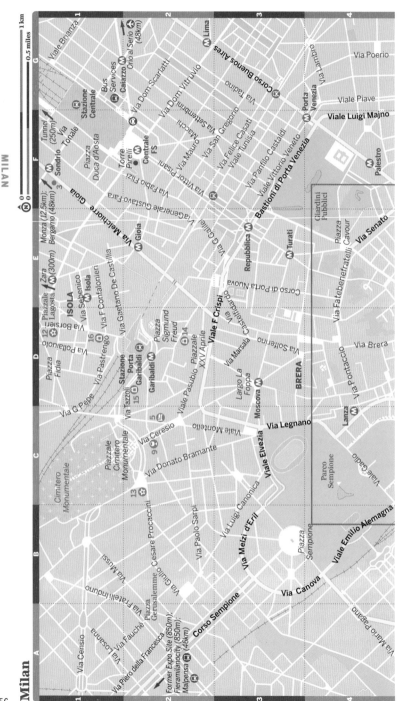

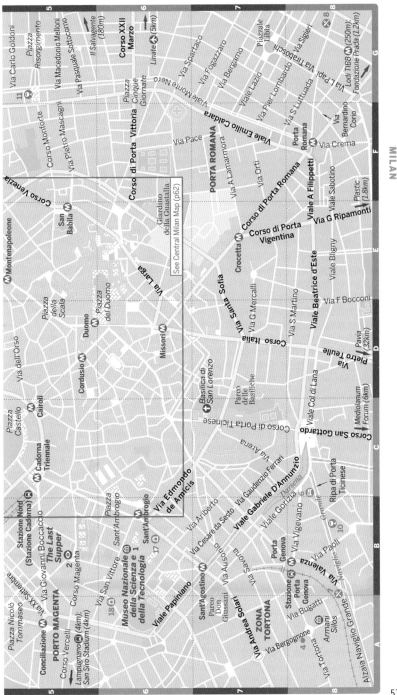

MILAN

Milan

a masterful psychological study and one of the world's most iconic images. To see it you must book in advance or sign up for a guided city tour.

★ Museo Nazionale della Scienza e della Tecnologia   MUSEUM
(Map p56; ☑02 48 55 51; www.museoscienza. org; Via San Vittore 21; adult/child €10/7, submarine tours €8; ⊙9.30am-5pm Tue-Fri, to 6.30pm Sat & Sun; 🚹; Ⓜ Sant'Ambrogio) Kids, would-be inventors and geeks will go goggle-eyed at Milan's impressive museum of science and technology, the largest of its kind in Italy. It is a fitting tribute in a city where arch-inventor Leonardo da Vinci did much of his finest work. The 16th-century monastery where it is housed features a collection of more than 10,000 items, including models based on da Vinci's engineering sketches, and outdoor hangars housing steam trains, planes, full-sized galleons and Italy's first submarine, *Enrico Toti*.

The museum's fabulous **MUST** Shop (Map p56; ☑02 4855 5340; www.mustshop.it; Via Olona 6; ⊙10am-7pm Tue-Sun; 🚹; Ⓜ Sant'Ambrogio) is the place for all manner of science-inspired books, design items, gadgets and games. Access it through the museum or from Via Olona.

Chiesa di San Maurizio   CHURCH
(Map p62; Corso Magenta 15; ⊙9.30am-5.30pm Tue-Sat, 1.30-5.30pm Sun; Ⓜ Cadorna) The 16th-century royal chapel and convent of San Maurizio is Milan's hidden crown jewel, every inch of it covered in breathtaking fres-

coes, several of them executed by Bernardino Luini who worked with Leonardo. Many of the frescoes immortalise Ippolita Sforza, Milanese literary maven, and other members of the powerful Sforza clan.

Basilica di Sant'Ambrogio   BASILICA
(Map p56; ☑02 8645 0895; www.basilicasant ambrogio.it; Piazza Sant'Ambrogio 15; ⊙10am-noon & 2.30-6pm Mon-Sat, 3-5pm Sun; Ⓜ Sant'Ambrogio) St Ambrose, Milan's patron saint and one-time superstar bishop, is buried in the crypt of this red-brick cathedral, which he founded in AD 379. It's a fitting legacy, built and rebuilt with a purposeful simplicity that is truly uplifting: the seminal Lombard Romanesque basilica. Shimmering altar mosaics and a biographical AD 835 golden altarpiece, which once served as the

---

❶ DIY TRAM TOURS

Enjoy your own city tour by hopping on **Tram No 1**. This retro orange beauty, complete with wooden seats and original fittings, runs along Via Settembrini before cutting through the historic centre along Via Manzoni, through Piazza Cordusio and back up towards Piazza Cairoli and the Castello Sforzesco. A 75-minute ticket (€1.50), which is also valid for the bus and metro, should be purchased from any tobacconist before boarding. Stamp it in the original *obliteratrice* on the tram.

MILAN SIGHTS

cladding for the saint's sarcophagus, light up the shadowy vaulted interior.

Fondazione Prada   GALLERY
(☑02 5666 2612; www.fondazioneprada.org; Largo Isarco 2; adult/reduced €10/8; ⊙10am-9pm; Ⓜ Lodi) Seven years in the making, the new Fondazione Prada, conceived by author and architect Miuccia Prada and Rem Koolhaas, is as innovative and creative as the minds that gave it shape. Seven renovated buildings and three new structures have transformed a dilapidated former brandy factory into 19,000 sq metres of exciting, multilevel exhibition space. The buildings, including a four-storey Haunted House tower clad in gold leaf, work seamlessly together, presenting some stunning visual perspectives.

🗫 Tours

Ad Artem   CULTURAL TOUR
(Map p56; ☑02 659 77 28; http://adartem. it; Via Melchiorre Gioia 1; tours €8-17.50; ⊙9am-1pm & 2-4pm; 🖈; Ⓜ Sondrio) Unusual cultural tours of Milan's museums and monuments with qualified art historians and actors. Highlight tours include a walk around the battlements of Castello Sforzesco; explorations of the castle's subterranean Ghirlanda passageway; and family-friendly tours of the Museo del Novecento, where kids are invited to build and design their own artwork.

★ **Città Nascosta Milano**   CULTURAL TOUR
(Map p62; ☑347 3661174; www.cittanascosta milano.it; Via del Bollo 3; annual membership €5-35; ⊙9.30am-1.30pm Mon-Fri, 2.30-6.30pm Tue & Thu; Ⓜ Duomo, Missori) Dedicated to showing you the hidden side of Milan, this nonprofit outfit runs exciting cultural tours. Previous offerings have lifted the curtain on Milan's Liberty tennis club, Casa Valerio and the emerging neighbourhood of Lambrate. Other themed programs include Einstein in Milan and the Interrupted Dream of Napoleon. It also runs multilingual tours during the annual Cortili Aperti.

Participation requires a small annual membership fee, which gives access to the tours, as well as those of affiliated organisations in Florence and Rome.

🎊 Festivals & Events

Milan has two linked trade-fair grounds, collectively known as **Fiera Milano** (www. fieramilano.it; Strada Statale del Sempione 28,

---

DON'T MISS

FEELING PECKISH?

Milan's historic deli is smaller than its reputation suggests, but what it lacks in space it makes up for in variety. It's home to a mind-boggling selection of *parmigiano reggiano* (Parmesan) and myriad other treasures – chocolates, pralines, pastries, freshly made gelato, seafood, caviar, pâté, fruit and vegetables, truffle products, olive oils and balsamic vinegars.

Peck also runs an all-day restaurant, **Peck Italian Bar** (Map p62; ☑02 869 30 17; www.peck.it; Via Cantù 3; meals €35-45; ⊙11.30am-9.30pm Mon-Sat; Ⓜ Duomo), which appeals to a banking and business lunch crowd. Like the clientele, the food is traditional and the service efficient.

Rho; Ⓜ Rho). The older of the two, **Fiera-milanocity**, is close to the centre (metro line 2, Lotto Fieramilanocity stop), while the main grounds, **Fieramilano**, are west of town in the satellite town of Rho (metro line 2, Rho Fiera stop). The furniture fair, fashion shows and most large trade fairs take place here.

Carnevale Ambrosiano   RELIGIOUS
Lent comes late to Milan, with Carnevale sensibly held on the Saturday that falls after everyone else's frantic February Fat Tuesday.

Salone Internazionale del Mobile   FAIR
(International Furniture Fair; www.salonemilano.it; ⊙Apr) The world's most prestigious furniture fair is held annually at Fiera Milano, with satellite exhibitions in Zona Tortona. Alongside the Salone runs the **Fuorisalone** (http://fuorisalone.it) – literally, the outdoor lounge – which incorporates dozens of spontaneous design-related events, parties, exhibits and shows that animate the entire city.

🛏 Sleeping

Great-value accommodation is hard to come by in Milan, particularly during the Salone del Mobile furniture fair, the fashion shows and other large fairs, at which time you should book months in advance. The tourist office distributes *Milano Hotels,* which lists more than 350 options.

★ Ostello Bello
HOSTEL €

(Map p62; ✆ 02 3658 2720; www.ostellobello.
com; Via Medici 4; dm €28-35, d €80-98, tr €110-
130; ❄ 🛜 📶; 🚇 2, 14) A breath of fresh air in
Milan's stiffly suited centre, this is the best
hostel in town. Entrance is through its lively bar-cafe, open to nonguests, where you're
welcomed with a smile and a complimentary
drink. Beds are in mixed dorms or spotless
private rooms, and there's a kitchen, a small
terrace, and a basement lounge equipped
with guitars, board games and table football.

Weekly events, including jam sessions,
cinema forums and a monthly vintage market, offer a great way to meet locals.

★ LaFavia Four Rooms
B&B €€

(Map p56; ✆ 347 7842212; http://lafavia
4rooms.com; Via Carlo Farini 4; s €90-105, d €100-
125; ❄ 🛜) Marco and Fabio's four-room
bed and breakfast in the former Rabarbaro
Zucca factory is a multicultural treat with
rooms inspired by their travels through
India, Mexico and Europe. Graphic wall-
papers by Manuela Canova in zippy greens
and oranges are complemented by lush
window views onto plant-filled verandahs.
Best of all is the rooftop garden where an
organic breakfast is served in summer.

★ Maison Borella
BOUTIQUE HOTEL €€

(Map p56; ✆ 02 5810 9114; www.hotelmaison
borella.com; Alzaia Naviglio Grande 8; d €160-280;
❄ @ 🛜; 🚇 Porta Genova) With geranium-clad
balconies overhanging the Naviglio Grande
and its striking black, white and grey decor,
this canalside hotel offers a touch of class
in a dedicated bohemian neighbourhood.
Converted from an old apartment building,
the hotel's rooms are arranged around an
internal courtyard and mix mid-century
and contemporary furnishings with period
features such as parquet floors, beamed
ceilings and elegant *boiserie* (sculpted pan-
elling).

Palazzo Segreti
DESIGN HOTEL €€

(Map p62; ✆ 02 4952 9250; www.palazzo
segreti.com; Via San Tomaso 8; d €180, ste
€250-350; ❄ 🛜; 🚇 Cairoli, Cordusio) This
19th-century palace of secrets hides a
shockingly modern interior and 18 subdued
rooms with raw concrete finishes, rough antique wooden floorboards and shadowy chi-
aroscuro lighting effects. It appeals to design
buffs who favour its minimal furnishings,
open-plan bathrooms and achingly hip bar

where folk gather in the evening to gossip
over goldfish-bowl-sized wine glasses.

✖ Eating

Milan's dining scene is much like its fashion
scene, with new restaurant openings hotly
debated and seats at Michelin-starred tables hard to come by. Whether it's dyed-in-
tradition or fusion cuisine you're after, you're
sure to eat some of Italy's most sophisticated
food here.

Mercato Metropolitano
ITALIAN €

(Map p56; www.mercatometropolitano.com;
Porta Genova; meals €10-20; ⊙ 11am-midnight
Mon-Thu, to 2am Fri, 9-2am Sat, 9am-noon Sun; 📶;
🚇 Porta Genova) 'Good Italian food is not a
luxury' is the cry of Milan's new food market located in former railway housings near
Porta Genova. Choose from small-producer
food stalls selling oysters, DOP Franciacorta, and gourmet *panini* made with 24-year-
aged San Daniele ham. Plant stalls, artisanal
ice-cream carts, craft beer, cocktail purvey-
ors, and even cooking classes and seminars
give it a convivial country-fair feel.

De Santis
SANDWICHES €

(Map p62; www.paninidesantis.it; Corso Magenta 9; sandwiches €6-8; ⊙ noon-11.30pm; 📶;
🚇 Cadorna) Sandwiches here are so damn
good you may eschew restaurant dining
just to sample that *panini* with prosciutto, spicy goat cheese, pepperoni, aubergine
and artichokes. The more than 200 varia-
tions on the menu and De Santis' decades
of experience explain the queues at this tiny
venue. Beer is served on tap to those who
find seating.

★ Un Posto a Milano
MODERN ITALIAN €€

(Map p56; ✆ 02 545 77 85; www.unposto
amilano.it; Via Cuccagna 2; meals €10-35; ⊙ 12.30-
3pm & 7.20-11pm Tue-Sun; ✎ 📶; 🚇 Porta Romana)
A few years ago this country *cascina* (farmhouse) was a derelict ruin, until a collection
of cooperatives and cultural associations
returned it to multifunctional use as restaurant, social hub and hostel. Delicious salads,
homemade focaccia, soups and snacks are
served throughout the day at the bar, while
the restaurant serves simple home cooking
using locally sourced ingredients.

Children are particularly welcome here.
High chairs are provided; there's a childrens'
menu and a lovely garden for postprandial
playing.

Trattoria Milanese
MILANESE €€

(Map p62; ☎02 8645 1991; Via Santa Marta 11; meals €30-45; ☺12.30-2.30pm & 7-11.30pm; 🚇2, 14) Like an old friend you haven't seen in years, this true trattoria welcomes you with generous goblets of wine, hearty servings of traditional Milanese fare and convivial banter over the vegetable buffet. Regulars slide into their favourite spots, barely needing to order as waiters bring them their usual: meatballs wrapped in cabbage, minestrone or the sinfully good *risotto al salto* (refried risotto).

★ La Brisa
MODERN ITALIAN €€€

(Map p62; ☎02 8645 0521; www.ristorantelabrisa.it; Via Brisa 15; meals €50-70; ☺12.45-2.30pm & 7.45-10.30pm Mon-Fri, 7.45-10.30pm Sun; 🚇Cairoli, Cordusio) Discreet, elegant and exquisitely romantic. Push open the screened door and the maître d' will guide you to a table beneath centuries-old linden trees in a secluded courtyard, where ivy climbs the walls and pink hydrangeas bob in the breeze. Chef Antonio Facciolo's seasonal menus are similarly elegant, his signature dish a mouthwatering roast pork in a myrtleberry drizzle.

🍷 Drinking & Nightlife

Milanese bars are generally open until 2am or 3am, and virtually all serve *aperitivi*. The Navigli canal district, the cobbled backstreets of Brera, and swish Corso Como are all drinking hot spots. Superstylish hotel and museum bars include Bar Luce at the Fondazione Prada, Armani Hotel's Bamboo Bar, the Bulgari bar, and the bar at 10 Corso Como.

Clubs are generally open until 3am or 4am from Tuesday to Sunday; cover charges vary from €10 to upwards of €25. Door policies can become formidable as the night wears on.

★ Ceresio 7
BAR

(Map p56; ☎02 3103 9221; www.ceresio7.com; Via Ceresio 7; aperitivo €15, meals €60-80; ☺12.30pm-1am; 🚇2, 4) Heady views match the heady price of *aperitivo* at Milan's coolest rooftop bar, sitting atop the former 1930s Enel (electricity company) HQ. Two pools, two bars and a restaurant under the guidance of former Bulgari head chef Elio Sironi make this a hit with Milan's beautiful people. In the summer you can book a whole day by the pool from €110.

Pasticceria Marchesi
CAFE

(Map p62; ☎02 87 67 30; www.pasticceriamarchesi.it; Via Santa Maria alla Porta 11a; ☺7.30am-8pm Tue-Sat, 8.30am-1pm Sun; 🚇Cardusio, Cairoli) Coffee that's perfect every shot since 1824, accompanied by a delectable array of sweets, biscuits and pastries.

Mag Café
BAR, CAFE

(Map p56; Ripa di Porta Ticinese 43; cocktails €7-9, brunch €10; ☺7.30-2am Mon-Fri, 9-2am Sat & Sun; 🚇2, 9) A Milanese speakeasy with armchairs in whisky-coloured velvet, marble-topped tables, a patchwork of Persian rugs and huge lampshades that look like birds' nests. Like the decor, the drinks are creatively crafted, utilising interesting herbs and syrups, and served in vintage glassware. Mag also does a popular brunch on weekends.

Nottingham Forest
COCKTAIL BAR

(Map p56; www.nottingham-forest.com; Viale Piave 1; cocktails €10; ☺6.30pm-2am Tue-Sat, 6pm-1am Sun; 🚇9, 23) If Michelin awarded stars for bars, Nottingham Forest would have a clutch of them. This eclectically decorated Asian-cum-African tiki bar named after an English football team is the outpost of molecular mixologist Dario Comino, who conjures smoking cocktails packed with dry ice and ingenuity. Unique cocktails include the Elite, a mix of vodka, ground pearls and sake – it's supposedly an aphrodisiac.

Central Milan

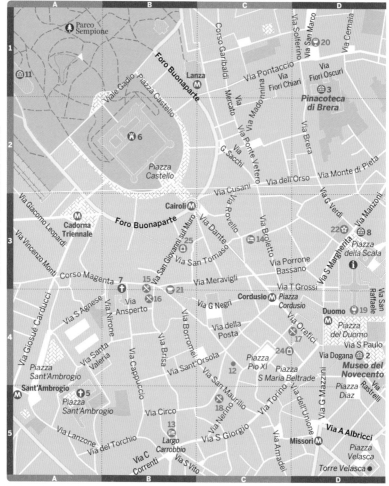

Camparino in Galleria BAR, CAFE
(Map p62; www.camparino.it; Piazza del Duomo 21; drinks €12-24; ⏰7.15am-8.40pm) Open since the inauguration of the Galleria Vittorio Emanuele II shopping arcade in 1867, this perfectly preserved art nouveau bar has served drinks to the likes of Verdi, Toscanini, Dudovich and Carrà. Cast-iron chandeliers, huge mirrored walls trimmed with wall mosaics of birds and flowers set the tone for a classy Campari-based *aperitivo*. Drinks at the bar are cheaper.

N'Ombra de Vin WINE BAR
(Map p62; ☑02 659 96 50; www.nombradevin.it; Via San Marco 2; ⏰10-2am; Ⓜ Lanza, Moscova) This *enoteca* (wine bar) is set in a one-time Augustine refectory. Tastings can be had all day and you can also indulge in food such as *carpaccio di pesce spade agli agrumi* (swordfish carpaccio prepared with citrus) from a limited menu. Check the website for occasional cultural events and DJ nights.

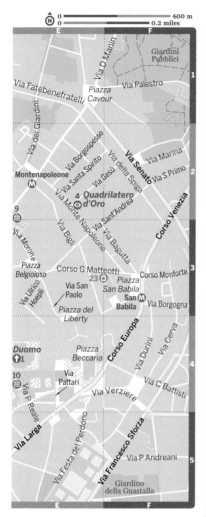

BEHIND THE SCENES AT LA SCALA

To glimpse the inner workings of La Scala, visit the **Ansaldo Workshops** (Map p56; ☑02 4335 3521; www.teatroalla scala.org; Via Bergognone 34; per person €5, groups €100-120; ☺individuals 3pm, groups 9am-noon & 2-4pm Tue & Thu; Ⓜ Porto Genova) where the stage sets are crafted and painted, and where some 800 to 1000 new costumes are handmade each season. Tours must be booked in advance and are guided by the heads of each creative department.

which run shuttle buses for concerts. They include **Mediolanum Forum** (☑02 48 85 71; www.mediolanumforum.it; Via Giuseppe di Vittorio 6; Ⓜ Assago Milanofiori) and the San Siro Stadium.

★ Teatro alla Scala   OPERA

(La Scala; Map p62; ☑02 8 87 91; www.teatroalla scala.org; Piazza della Scala; Ⓜ Duomo) One of the most famous opera stages in the world, La Scala's season runs from early December through July. You can also see theatre, ballet and concerts here year-round (except August). Buy tickets online or by phone up to two months before the performance, and then from the central **box office** (☑02 72 00 37 44; www.teatroallascala.org; Galleria Vittorio Emanuele II; ☺noon-6pm; Ⓜ Duomo).

Blue Note   JAZZ

(Map p56; ☑02 6901 6888; www.bluenote milano.com; Via Borsieri 37; tickets €22-40; ☺7.30pm-midnight Tue-Sun Sep-Jun, brunch noon Sun Oct-Mar; Ⓜ Isola, Zara) Top-class jazz acts from around the world perform here at the only European outpost for New York's Blue Note jazz club. If you haven't prebooked you can buy tickets at the door from 7.30pm. It also does a popular easy-listening Sunday brunch (€35 per adult, or €70 for two adults and two children under 12).

La Fabbrica del Vapore   PERFORMING ARTS

(Map p56; www.fabbricadelvapore.org; Via Procaccini 4; ✆; ☐7, 12, 14) This industrial site once housed a factory for electric trams; now it lends its vast warehouses to a centre of the arts particularly aimed at developing the creative skills of young people. Dance, photography, theatre, cinema and concerts fill the factory's program year-round.

Plastic   CLUB

(Via Gargano 15; ☺11pm-5am Fri-Sat, to 3am Sun; ☐24) A legendary club still going strong after 30 years. Madonna, Amy Winehouse, Blur and a whole host of other big names have performed here alongside more transgressive acts, attracting a mixed crowd of creatives and Milan's coolest kids. You'll find it just south of the Lodi metro stop just off Viale Brenta. No door charge.

☆ Entertainment

Most big events and names that play Milan do so at major venues outside the city centre,

Central Milan

San Siro Stadium FOOTBALL
(Stadio Giuseppe Meazza; www.sansiro.net; Piazzale Angelo Moratti, museum & tours gate 14; tickets from €20; MSan Siro) San Siro Stadium wasn't designed to hold the entire population of Milan, but on a Sunday afternoon amid 85,000 football-mad citizens it can certainly feel like it. The city's two clubs, AC Milan and FC Internazionale Milano (aka Inter), play on alternate weeks from October to May.

🛍 Shopping

Beyond the hallowed streets of the Quadrilatero d'Oro, designer outlets and chains can be found along Corso Buenos Aires and Corso Vercelli; younger, hipper labels live along Via Brera and Corso Magenta; while Corso di Porta Ticinese and Navigli are home of the Milan street scene and subculture shops.

★**Spazio Rossana Orlandi** HOMEWARES
(Map p56; ☑02 46 74 47; www.rossanaorlandi.com; Via Matteo Bandello 14; ☺3-7pm Mon, 10am-7pm Tue-Sat; MSant'Ambrogio) Installed in a former tie factory in the Magenta district, this iconic interior design studio is a challenge to find. Once inside, though, it's hard to leave this treasure trove stacked with vintage and contemporary limited-edition pieces from upcoming artists.

Monica Castiglioni JEWELLERY
(Map p56; ☑02 8723 7979; www.monicacastiglioni.com; Via Pastrengo 4; ☺11am-8pm Thu-Sat; MGaribaldi) Daughter of famous industrial designer Achille Castiglioni, Monica Castiglioni has a deep understanding of materials and proportions. To this she adds her own unique vision, turning out organic, industrial-style jewellery in bronze, silver and gold using an ancient lost-wax casting technique.

Moroni Gomma HOMEWARES, ACCESSORIES
(Map p62; ☑02 79 62 20; www.moronigomma.it; Corso Matteotti 14; ☺3-7pm Mon, 10am-7pm Tue-Sun; MSan Babila) Stocked with irresistible gadgets and great accessories for the bathroom, kitchen and office, this family-owned design store is a one-stop shop for funky souvenirs and Milanese keepsakes. Who but the strongest willed will be able to resist the cuckoo clock shaped like the Duomo, a retro telephone in pastel colours or classic Italian moccasins in nonslip rubber?

Risi FASHION
(Map p62; ☑02 8909 2185; www.risimilano.com; Via San Giovanni sul Muro 21; ☺3-7.30pm Mon, 10am-2.30pm & 3-7.30pm Tue-Sat; MCairoli) Head to Risi for a dose of effortless Milanese chic. Here you can stock up on soft grey and white linen shirts and trousers, honeycomb polo shirts in sober colours and comfortable beachwear in classic pinstripes. Season-

MILAN SHOPPING

appropriate weights and an absence of logos mean you'll blend in with the natives.

10 Corso Como FASHION
(Map p56; ☑02 2900 2674; www.10corso como.com; Corso Como 10; ⊙10.30am-7.30pm Tue & Fri-Sun, to 9pm Wed & Thu, 3.30-7.30pm Mon; MGaribaldi) This might be the world's most hyped 'concept shop', but Carla Sozzani's selection of desirable things (Lan-vin ballet flats, Alexander Girard wooden dolls, a demicouture frock by a designer you've not read about *yet*) makes 10 Corso Como a fun window-shopping experience. There's a bookshop upstairs with art and design titles, and a hyper-stylish bar and restaurant in the main atrium and picture-perfect courtyard.

Bargain hunters take note: the **out-let store** (Map p56; ☑02 2900 2674; www .10corsocomo.com; Via Tazzoli 3; ⊙1-7pm Fri, 11am-7pm Sat & Sun; MGaribaldi, ☐3, 4) nearby sells last season's stock at a discount.

ⓘ Information

EMERGENCY
Police Station (Questura; ☑02 6 22 61; Via Fatebenefratelli 11; ⊙8am-2pm & 3-8pm Mon-Fri, 8am-2pm Sat; MTurati) Milan's main police station.

MEDICAL SERVICES
24-Hour Pharmacy (☑02 669 07 35; Galleria delle Partenze, Stazione Centrale; ⊙7.30am-8.30pm; MCentrale FS) Located on the 1st floor of the central station.

American International Medical Centre (AIMC; ☑02 5831 9808; www.aimclinic.it; Via Mercalli 11; MCrocetta) Private, international health clinic with English-speaking staff.

Ospedale Maggiore Policlinico (☑02 5503 6672; www.policlinico.mi.it; Via Francesco Sforza 35; MCrocetta) Milan's main hospital; offers an outpatient service.

TOURIST INFORMATION
Milan Tourist Office (Map p62; ☑02 8845 6555; www.turismo.milano.it; Galleria Vittorio Emanuele II 11-12; ⊙9am-7pm Mon-Fri, to 6pm Sat, 10am-6pm Sun; MDuomo) Centrally located with helpful English-speaking staff and tons of maps and brochures.

DON'T MISS

QUADRILATERO D'ORO

A stroll around the **Quadrilatero d'Oro** (Golden Quad; Map p62; Ⓜ Monte Napoleone), the world's most famous shopping district, is a must. This quaint-ly cobbled quadrangle of streets – bounded by Via Monte Napoleone, Via Sant'Andrea, Via della Spiga and Via Alessandro Manzoni – has always been synonymous with elegance and money (Via Monte Napoleone was where Na-poleon's government managed loans). Even if you don't have the slightest urge to sling a swag of glossy carriers, the window displays and people-watching are priceless.

ⓘ Getting There & Away

CAR & MOTORCYCLE
The A1, A4, A7 and A8 converge from all directions on Milan.

ⓘ Getting Around

CAR & MOTORCYCLE
It simply isn't worth having a car in Milan. Many streets have restricted access and parking is a nightmare. In the centre, street parking costs €2 per hour. To pay, buy a SostaMilano card from a tobacconist, scratch off the date and hour, and display it on your dashboard. Only park in the blue spaces; those marked in yellow are reserved for residents. Underground car parks charge between €25 and €40 for 24 hours. Check out www.tuttoc-itta.it/parcheggi/milano to find one near you.

PUBLIC TRANSPORT
ATM (Azienda Trasporti Milano; ☑02 4860 7607; www.atm.it) Runs the metro, buses and trams. The metro is the most convenient way to get around and consists of four underground lines (red M1, green M2, yellow M3 and lilac M5) and a suburban rail network, the blue Passante Ferroviario. Services run from 6am to 12.30am. A ticket costs €1.50 and is valid for one metro ride or up to 90 minutes' travel on buses and trams.

Beyond Milan pretty countryside unfolds, dotted with patrician towns; all are steeped in history, hiding fabulous Unesco monuments and world-class museums. To the north a burst of Mediterranean colour and a balmy microclimate awaits around Lakes Orta, Maggiore, Como, Garda and Iseo. No wonder George Clooney is smitten.

Around Milan

Lago Maggiore

Even in this region of breathtaking beauty, Lake Maggiore shines. Its wide waters reflect mountains that are often snow-topped; its shores are lined with rich architectural reminders of a grand 19th-century past. And it boasts the beguiling palace-dotted Borromean Islands, which, like a fleet of fine vessels, lie at anchor in the Borromean Gulf.

❶ Information

The website www.illagomaggiore.com features lake-wide information.

Stresa

POP 5000

Stresa's easy accessibility from Milan has long made it a favourite among writers and artists, and today its sunny lake-front promenades are backed by architectural reminders of its heyday. Among the high-profile visitors to Stresa was author Ernest Hemingway. In 1918 he recovered from a war wound here, and set some pivotal scenes of *A Farewell to Arms* at the Grand Hôtel des Iles Borromées – which remains the most palatial of the hotels garlanding the lake.

◉ Sights & Activities

Giardino Botanico Alpinia   GARDENS
(⏰ 0323 3 02 95; adult/reduced €3/2.50; ⏰ 9.30am-6pm Apr-Oct) More than 1000 Alpine and sub-Alpine species flourish in this 4-hectare botanical garden set part-way up Monte Mottarone. It was founded in 1934 and profiles trees and shrubs from as far away as China and Japan against a backdrop of fine lake views. If the Stresa–Mottarone cable car is operating, the easiest access is via the Alpino midstation. Otherwise, the gardens are a 10km drive from Stresa; check whether the bus is running from the tourist office (single €3; 30 minutes).

Funivia Stresa–Mottarone   CABLE CAR
(⏰ 0323 3 02 95; www.stresa-mottarone.it; Piazzale della Funivia; return adult/reduced €13.50/8.50, to Alpino station €8/5.50; ⏰ 9.30am-5.30pm Apr-Oct, 8.10am-5.30pm Nov-Mar) Captivating lake views unfold during a 20-minute cable-car journey to the top of 1491m-high Monte Mottarone. On a clear day you can see Lago Maggiore, Lago d'Orta and Monte Rosa on the Swiss border. At the Alpino midstation a profusion of Alpine plants flourish in the Giardino Botanico Alpinia. The mountain itself offers good hiking and biking trails. At time of writing the cable car was closed for repairs; a re-opening date had not yet been set.

🛏 Sleeping

There are some 40 campgrounds along Maggiore's western shore; the tourist office has a list. Seasonal closings (including hotels) are generally from November to February, but this can vary; check ahead.

Hotel Saini Meublè
HOTEL €

(☑ 0323 93 45 19; www.hotelsaini.it; Via Garibaldi 10; s €70-94, d €72-112) With their warm tones, and wooden cabinets and floors, the rooms in Hotel Saini have a timeless feel – fitting for a house that's some 400 years old. Spacious bedrooms, a swirling spiral staircase and a location in the heart of the old town add to the appeal.

Villa e Palazzo Aminta
HOTEL €€€

(☑ 0323 93 38 18; www.villa-aminta.it; Via Sempione Nord 123; d €235-500, ste €640-1125; P ✳ ⓢ ⛱) Luxuriate in turn-of-the-century style at Villa Aminta, which offers picture-perfect views of an island-studded lake. Rooms decked out with Murano chandeliers, silk curtains, and acres of velvet and gilt echo the opulence of Stresa's belle époque. The hotel also has its own private beach, heated pool and fitness centre.

✗ Eating & Drinking

Taverna del Pappagallo
TRATTORIA €

(☑ 0323 3 04 11; www.tavernapappagallo.com; Via Principessa Margherita 46; meals €20-25; ⊙ 6.30-11pm Thu-Tue) It's not fancy and it's not super serious but this welcoming backstreet trattoria is where you'll find Stresa's families tucking into tasty regional dishes ranging from pizzas cooked in an old wood-fired oven to risotto with lake fish.

The clams with homemade pasta are positively steeped in garlic and white wine.

★ Piemontese
PIEDMONTESE €€

(☑ 0323 3 02 35; www.ristorantepiemontese.com; Via Mazzini 25; meals €35-45; ⊙ 12.30-2pm & 6.30-9.30pm) The name gives a huge clue as to the focus of this refined *ristorante*. Regional delights include gnocchi with gorgonzola and hazelnuts; cold veal with tuna sauce; and risotto made using Piedmont's own Barolo wine. The Lake Menu (€34) features carp, trout, perch and pike, while the set lunch menu is a steal (two/three courses €23/28).

Grand Hotel des Iles
Borromées
COCKTAIL BAR

(☑ 0323 93 89 38; www.borromees.it; Corso Umberto I 67; ⊙ 6pm-late) Following his WWI stint on the Italian front, Ernest Hemingway checked in here to nurse his battle scars, and to write *A Farewell to Arms*. The passionate antiwar novel featured this sumptuous hotel. You might baulk at room prices (guests have included Princess Margaret and the Vanderbilts) but you can still

DOUG PEARSON/GETTY IMAGES ©

View of Isola Bella

slug back a Manhattan on the terraces with cinematic views.

❶ Information

Stresa Tourist Office (☑ 0323 3 13 08; www.stresaturismo.it; Piazza Marconi 16; ⊙ 10am-12.30pm & 3-6.30pm summer, reduced hours winter)

Borromean Islands

The Borromean Gulf forms Lago Maggiore's most beautiful corner, sheltering as it does the palaces and gardens of the Borromean Islands. These can be reached from various points around the lake, but Stresa and the village of Baveno (3km to the north) offer the best access.

ISOLA BELLA

Isola Bella was named after Isabella, wife of Carlo Borromeo III, when the island's centrepiece Palazzo Borromeo was built for the aristocratic family in the 17th century. Both villa and gardens were designed to lend the whole island the appearance of a ship, with the villa at the prow and the gardens dripping down terraces at the rear.

◉ Sights

★ Palazzo Borromeo
PALACE

(☑ 0323 3 05 56; www.isoleborromee.it; Isola Bella; adult/child €15/8.50, incl Palazzo Madre €21/10; ⊙ 9am-5.30pm mid-Mar–mid-Oct) Presiding over 10 tiers of spectacular terraced gardens roamed by peacocks, this baroque palace is arguably Lago Maggiore's finest building. Wandering the ground and 1st floors reveals guest rooms, studies and reception halls. Particularly striking rooms include the Sala di Napoleone, where the emperor Napoleon stayed with his wife in 1797; the grand Sala da Ballo (Ballroom); the ornate Sala del Trono (Throne Room); and the Sala delle Regine (Queen's Room). Paintings from a 130-strong Borromeo collection hang all around.

A combined ticket also covers admission to Palazzo Madre on nearby Isola Madre.

✕ Eating

Elvezia ITALIAN €€
(☑0323 3 00 43; Via Vittorio Emanuele 18; meals €30-35; ☺noon-2pm & 6.30-9pm Tue-Sun Mar-Oct, Fri-Sun only Nov-Feb) With its rambling rooms, fish-themed portico and upstairs pergola and balcony dining area, this is the best spot on Isola Bella for home cooking. Dishes include ricotta-stuffed ravioli, various risottos and lake fish such as *coregone alle mandorle* (lake whitefish in almonds).

ISOLA MADRE

⭐**Palazzo Madre** PALACE
See p19.

ISOLA SUPERIORE (PESCATORI)

Although it lacks any specific sights, tiny Fishermen's Island retains much of its original village atmosphere. A huddle of streets shelters the **Chiesa di San Vittore**, which has an 11th-century apse and a 16th-century fresco, but the real reasons to visit are the island's restaurants, which specialise in grilled fish.

🛏 Sleeping & Eating

⭐**Albergo Verbano** HOTEL €€
(☑0323 3 04 08; www.hotelverbano.it; Via Ugo Ara 2; s €70-170, d €80-230; ☺Mar-Dec; 🛜) Set at the southern tip of enchanting Isola Superiore, Albergo Verbano has been putting up guests in this idyllic spot since 1895. Dishes from a fish-focused menu are served on the tree-shaded waterside terrace, and bedrooms are a study in unstuffy elegance – choose one looking out towards Isola Bella or Isola Madre; the views are exquisite either way.

⭐**Casabella** RISTORANTE €€€
(☑0323 3 34 71; www.isola-pescatori.it; Via del Marinaio 1; meals €30-50, 5-course tasting menu

€55; ☺noon-2pm & 6-8.30pm Feb-Nov) The setting is bewitching – right by the shore – and the food is acclaimed. The admirably short menu might feature home-smoked beef with spinach, blanched squid with ricotta or perfectly cooked lake fish. Leave room for dessert; the pear cake with chocolate fondant is faultless.

If you don't want to leave after dinner (likely) there are two snug bedrooms on site.

Verbania
POP 31,100

Sprawling Verbania is split into three districts. Of these, Verbania Pallanza is the most interesting, with a tight web of lanes in its old centre. Verbania Intra has a pleasant waterfront backed by elegant houses, and provides handy car ferries to Laveno on the eastern shore.

⊙ Sights

Villa Taranto GARDENS
See p20.

🛏 Sleeping

Aquadolce HOTEL €
(☑0323 50 54 18; www.hotelaquadolce.it; Via Cietti 1, Verbania Pallanza; s €70, d €95-105; ❄🛜) Ask for a room at the front of this bijou waterfront address and your window will be filled with a glittering lake backed by the mountains rearing up behind. Inside it's a beautifully lit, genteel affair, with all the quiet assurance of a well-run hotel.

✕ Eating

⭐**Osteria Castello** OSTERIA €€
(☑0323 51 65 79; www.osteriacastello.com; Piazza Castello 9, Verbania Intra; meals €25; ☺11am-3pm & 6pm-midnight, closed Sun) Its 100-plus years of history run like a rich seam through this enchanting *osteria,* where archive photos and bottles line the walls. Order a glass of wine from the vast selection, sample some ham, or tuck into the pasta or lake fish.

⭐**Ristorante Milano** MODERN ITALIAN €€€
(☑0323 55 68 16; www.ristorantemilanolago maggiore.it; Corso Zanitello 2, Verbania Pallanza; meals €50-70; ☺noon-2pm & 7-9pm Wed-Sun, noon-2pm Mon) The setting really is hard to beat: Milano directly overlooks Pallanza's minuscule horseshoe-shaped harbour (200m south of the ferry jetty); a scattering of tables sits on lakeside lawns amid the

trees. It's an idyllic spot to enjoy lake fish, local lamb and some innovative Italian cuisine, such as *risotto ai petali di rosa* (risotto with rose petals).

ℹ Information

Verbania Tourist Office (☑ 0323 50 32 49; www.verbania-turismo.it; Corso Zanitello 6, Verbania Pallanza; ⊘9am-1pm Mon-Fri)

Cannobio

POP 5140

Sheltered by a high mountain at the foot of the Val Cannobino, the medieval hamlet of Cannobio, just 5km from the Swiss border, is a dreamy place with some of the best restaurants and hotels on Lake Maggiore.

🏃 Activities

Tomaso Surf & Sail   WATER SPORTS
(☑ 333 7000291; www.tomaso.com; Via Nazionale 7) Offers lessons in windsurfing (per hour €75), sailing (per hour €105) and water-skiing (per half-hour €85). Experienced water-sports enthusiasts can also rent equipment (windsurf board and rig per one/four hours €22/70; sailing dinghy per one/two hours €35/55).

🛏 Sleeping & Eating

★ Hotel Pironi   HOTEL €€
See p20.

Lo Scalo   MODERN ITALIAN €€
(☑ 0323 7 14 80; www.loscalo.com; Piazza Vittorio Emanuele III 32; meals €35-45; ⊘noon-2.30pm & 6-9pm Wed-Sun, 6-9pm Tue) The pick of the restaurants along the main promenade, elegant Lo Scalo serves cuisine that is sophisticated and precise, featuring dishes such as an inky-black ravioli with squid and a pea and bergamot sauce. The set two-course lunch (€25) and five-course *menù degustazione* (€50) are both great-value treats.

ℹ Information

Tourist Office (☑ 0323 7 12 12; www.pro cannobio.it; Via Giovanola 25; ⊘9am-noon & 4-7pm Mon-Sat, 9am-noon Sun)

Lago d'Orta

Shrouded by thick, dark-green woodlands and backed by Monte Mottarone, little Lago d'Orta is just 13.4km long and 2.5km wide. The key points of the lake are the medieval

---

VAL CANNOBINO

To explore the wildly beautiful valley that winds northwest out of Cannobio, take the scenic SP75. It snakes for 28km beside a waterway via heavily wooded hills to Malesco in Valle Vigezzo. Just 2.5km along the valley, in Sant'Anna, the powerful Torrente Cannobino forces its way through a narrow gorge known as the Orrido di Sant'Anna, crossed at its narrowest part by a Romanesque bridge. A further 7km on, a steep 3km side road leads, via switchbacks and hairpin bends, up to the central valley's main town, Falmenta. Hire mountain bikes in Cannobio from Cicli Prezan (☑ 0323 7 12 30; www.cicliprezan.it; Viale Vittorio Veneto 9; per hr/day €10/20; ⊘8.30am-noon & 3-7pm Mon-Sat, 8.30pm-noon Sun).

---

village of Orta San Giulio and the Isola San Giulio, which sits just offshore.

◉ Sights

Orta San Giulio Old Town   AREA
The medieval village of Orta San Giulio (population just 1150), often referred to simply as Orta, is the focal point of Lago d'Orta and is the lake's main village. At its heart the central square, Piazza Motta, is framed by cream-coloured houses roofed with thick slate tiles. It's overlooked by the Palazotto, a frescoed 16th-century building borne up by stilts above a small loggia.

Basilica di San Giulio   CHURCH
(⊘9.30am-6pm Tue-Sun, 2-5pm Mon Apr-Sep, 9.30am-noon & 2-5pm Tue-Sun, 2-5pm Mon Oct-Mar) Isola San Giulio is dominated at its south end by the 12th-century Basilica di San Giulio, which is full of vibrant frescoes that alone make a trip to the island worthwhile. The church, island and mainland town are named after a Greek evangelist, Giulio, who's said to have rid the island of snakes, dragons and assorted monsters in the late 4th century. Regular ferries shuttle between the island and Orta San Giulio.

Sacro Monte di San Francesco CHAPEL, PARK
Beyond the lush gardens and residences that mark the hill rising behind Orta is a kind of parallel 'town' – the *sacro monte,* where 20 small chapels dedicated to St Francis of

Statue at Villa Olmo (p21), Como

Assisi dot the hillside. The views down the lake are captivating, and meandering from chapel to chapel is a wonderfully tranquil way to pass a few hours.

🛏 Sleeping

★Locanda di Orta   BOUTIQUE HOTEL €
(📞0322 90 51 88; www.locandaorta.com; Via Olina 18, Orta San Giulio; s €65-70, d €85-90, ste €150-160; 🛜) Teaming white leather and bold pink beside medieval grey stone walls is a bold design choice – but it works. Because of the age and size of the building, the cheaper rooms are tiny, but still delightful. Suites are roomier; each features a jacuzzi and a pocket-sized balcony overlooking the cobbled lane.

🍴 Eating

Enoteca Al Boeuc   PIEDMONTESE €
(📞339 5840039; http://alboeuc.beepworld. it; Via Bersani 28, Orta San Giulio; meals €15-20; 🕐11.30am-3pm & 6.30pm-midnight Wed-Mon) This candlelit stone cavern has been around since the 16th century. These days it offers glasses of fine wines (try the velvety Barolo for €8) and snacks including mixed bruschette with truffles and mushrooms, meat and cheese platters, and that Piedmontese favourite: *bagna caüda* (a hot dip of butter, olive oil, garlic and anchovies in which you bathe vegetables).

Cucchiaio di Legno   AGRITURISMO €
(📞339 5775385; www.ilcucchiaiodilegno.com; Via Prisciola 10, Orta San Giulio; set menu €24; 🕐6-9pm Thu-Sun, noon-2.30pm Sat & Sun; 🅿🛜) Delicious home cooking emerges from the kitchen of this honest-to-goodness *agriturismo* (farm stay accommodation); expect fish fresh from the lake, and salami and cheese from the surrounding valleys. When eating alfresco on the vine-draped patio it feels rather like you're dining at the house of a friend. Bookings required.

There's a clutch of bright, snazzy rooms too (doubles €80). It's 800m from the Orta–Miasino train station.

★Locanda di Orta   MODERN ITALIAN €€€
(📞0322 90 51 88; www.locandaorta.com; Via Olina 18, Orta San Giulio; meals €50; 🕐noon-2.30pm & 7.30-9pm) Tiny Orta can now boast its very own Michelin star – in the wisteria-draped Locanda di Orta, squeezed into the heart of the old town. It's a supremely stylish, intimate affair (it only seats around 17 people) where culinary alchemy converts traditional Lago d'Orta ingredients into works of foodie art.

The 250-strong wine list is also impressive.

ℹ Information

Main Tourist Office (📞0322 90 51 63; www. distrettolaghi.it; Via Panoramica, Orta San Giulio; 🕐10am-12.30pm & 2.30-5.30pm Mon-Thu, 11am-1pm & 2.30-6.30pm Fri-Sun) Can provide information on the whole of Lago d'Orta.

Pro Loco (📞0322 9 01 55; Via Bossi 11, Orta San Giulio; 🕐11am-1pm & 2-4pm Mon, Tue & Thu, 10am-1pm & 2-4pm Fri-Sun) Tourist information office in the town hall.

Lago di Como

Set in the shadow of the snow-covered Rhaetian Alps and hemmed in by steep, wooded hills, Lago di Como (also known as Lago di Lario) is the most spectacular of the region's three main lakes. Shaped like an upside-down letter Y, its winding shoreline is dotted with ancient villages and exquisite villas.

The lake's main town, Como, sits where the southern and western shores converge.

🎉 Festivals

Lake Como Festival   MUSIC
(www.lakecomofestival.com; 🕐May & Jun) Musical concerts are held at some of Lago di Como's finest villas.

ℹ Information

The website www.lakecomo.it features information covering the whole lake.

ℹ Getting There & Around

From Milan, take the A9 motorway, turning off at Monte Olimpino for Como. The SS36 leads east to Lecco while the SS233 heads west to Varese. The roads around the lake are superbly scenic, but also windy, narrow and busy in summer.

Como

POP 84,900

With its lively historic centre, 12th-century city walls and a self-confident air, Como is an elegant and prosperous town. Built on the wealth of the silk industry, its pedestrianised core is chock-full of bars, restaurants and places to sleep, making the town an ideal southern Lago di Como base.

⊙ Sights

Passeggiata Lino Gelpi   WATERFRONT
One of Como's most charming walks is the lakeside stroll west from Piazza Cavour. Passeggiata Lino Gelpi leads past the **Monumento ai Caduti** (Memorial; Viale Puecher 9), a 1931 memorial to Italy's WWI dead and a classic example of Fascist-era architecture. Next you'll pass a series of mansions and villas, including **Villa Saporiti** and **Villa Gallia**, both now owned by the provincial government and closed to the public, before arriving at the garden-ringed Villa Olmo.

Villa Olmo   HISTORIC BUILDING
See p21.

★ Duomo   CATHEDRAL
(Piazza del Duomo; ⊙ 7.30am-7.30pm Mon-Sat, to 9.30pm Sun) Although largely Gothic in style, elements of Romanesque, Renaissance and baroque can also be seen in Como's imposing, marble-clad *duomo*. The cathedral was built between the 14th and 18th centuries, and is crowned by a high octagonal dome.

★ Basilica di San Fedele   BASILICA
(Piazza San Fedele; ⊙ 8am-noon & 3.30-7pm) With three naves and three apses, this evocative basilica is often likened to a clover leaf. Parts of it date from the 6th century while the facade is the result of a 1914 revamp. The 16th-century rose window and 16th- and 17th-century frescoes enhance the appeal. The apses are centuries-old and feature some eye-catching sculpture on the right.

Museo della Seta   MUSEUM
See p21.

⊼ Activities

★ Lido di Villa Olmo   SWIMMING
(✆ 031 57 08 71; www.lidovillaolmo.it; Via Cernobbio 2; adult/reduced €7/3.50; ⊙ 9am-7pm mid-May–Sep) What a delight: a compact *lido* (beach) where you can plunge into open-air pools, sunbathe beside the lake, rent boats, sip cocktails at the waterfront bar and soak up mountain views. Bliss.

★ Aero Club Como   SCENIC FLIGHTS
(✆ 031 57 44 95; www.aeroclubcomo.com; Viale Masia 44; 30 min flight from €140) For a true touch of glamour, take one of these seaplane tours and buzz about the skies high above Como. The often-bumpy take-off and landing on the lake itself is thrilling, as are the views down onto the miniature villas and villages dotted far below. Flights are popular; in summer book three or four days ahead.

Funicolare Como–Brunate   CABLE CAR
(✆ 031 30 36 08; www.funicolarecomo.it; Piazza de Gasperi 4; adult one way/return €3/5.50, reduced €2/3.20; ⊙ half-hourly departures 8am-midnight summer, to 10.30pm winter) Prepare for some spectacular views. The Como–Brunate cable car (built in 1894) takes seven minutes to trundle up to the quiet hilltop village of Brunate (720m), revealing a memorable panorama of mountains and lakes. From there a steep 30-minute walk along a stony mule track leads to San Maurizio (907m), where 143 steps climb to the top of a lighthouse.

🛏 Sleeping

★ Quarcino   HOTEL €
(✆ 031 30 39 34; www.hotelquarcino.it; Salita Quarchino 4; s/d/tr/q €57/80/115/130; P ❋ 🖗) You'll struggle to find a more appealing, central budget hotel in Como. The modern decor is simple but stylish, the bathrooms are pristine and there are lake glimpses from many of the front rooms.

★ Avenue Hotel   BOUTIQUE HOTEL €€
(✆ 031 27 21 86; www.avenuehotel.it; Piazzolo Terragni 6; d €170-240, ste from €340; P ❋ 🖗) An assured sense of style at this delightful

Como

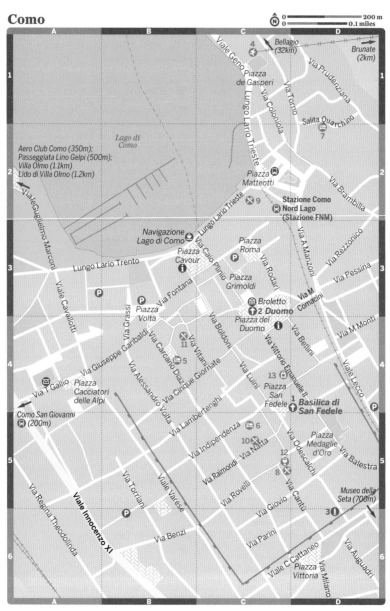

hotel sees ultramodern, minimalist rooms team crisp white walls with shots of purple or fuchsia-pink. Breakfast is served in a chic courtyard, service is warm but discreet and you can borrow a bike for free.

Albergo del Duca   HOTEL **€€**

(☏ 031 26 48 59; www.albergodelduca.it; Piazza Mazzini 12; s €60-75, d €100-130) The setting is an attractive one (on the edge of a pedestrianised square), the atmosphere is all friendliness,

Como

and the rooms are as neat as a pin, with polished wooden floors.

Eating & Drinking

Como's food market (☉8.30am-1pm Tue & Thu, to 7pm Sat) is held outside Porta Torre (Map p60).

★Natta Café
CAFE €

(☑031 26 91 23; www.nattacafe.com; Via Natta 16; meals €15-20; ☉12.30-3pm & 6.30pm-midnight Tue-Sat, 12.30-3pm & 7.30-11.30pm Sun; ☎) It's almost as if this is an *osteria* for the next generation. Yes, there's a proud focus on superb local ingredients and classic wines, but this laid-back cafe also has a beatnik atmosphere. So you get Chianti on the wine list, risotto with lake perch on the menu and Edith Piaf on the soundtrack. One cool vibe.

Castiglioni
TRATTORIA €

(☑031 26 33 88; www.castiglionistore.com; Via Cantù 9; meals €20; ☉8am-2.30pm & 4-7pm Mon-Fri, 8am-7.30pm Sun) Going strong since 1958, Castiglioni's wonderful deli has evolved to include a wine bar and now a restaurant. Sample dozens of local vintages with plates of sweet prosciutto, or take lunch on the pleasant outdoor patio. The menu, which includes all manner of charcuterie plates, lake fish and mountain meat dishes, is surprisingly refined and great value.

Gelateria Ceccato
GELATERIA €

(☑031 2 33 91; Lungo Lario Trieste 16; gelato €2-4; ☉noon-midnight summer, hours vary winter) For generations *comaschi* (people from Como) have turned to Ceccato for their Sunday-afternoon gelato and then embarked on a ritual *passeggiata* (stroll) with their dripping cones along the lakeshore. You can do

no better than imitate them: order a creamy *stracciatella* (chocolate chip) or perhaps a mix of fresh fruit flavours and head off for a relaxed promenade.

★Osteria del Gallo
ITALIAN €€

(☑031 27 25 91; www.osteriadelgallo-como.it; Via Vitani 16; meals €25-30; ☉12.30-3pm Mon, to 9pm Tue-Sat) An ageless *osteria* that looks exactly the part. In the wood-lined dining room, wine bottles and other goodies fill the shelves, and diners sit at small timber tables to tuck into traditional local food. The menu is chalked up daily and might include a first course of *zuppa di ceci* (chickpea soup), followed by lightly fried lake fish.

Enoteca Castiglioni
WINE BAR

(☑031 26 18 60; www.castiglionistore.com; Via Rovelli 17; ☉10am-8pm Mon-Fri, to 9pm Sun) If you're lucky you'll bag one of the clutch of tiny tables beside the ranks of wine-bottle lined shelves. It's a smart, modern setting in which to sample top-quality deli produce along with first-rate vintages.

Shopping

A weekly craft and antiques market (Piazza San Fedele; ☉9am-7pm Sat) fills the piazza beside the Basilica di San Fedele.

A Picci
GIFTS

(☑031 26 13 69; Via Vittorio Emanuele II 54; ☉3-7.30pm Mon, 9am-12.30pm & 3-7.30pm Tue-Sat) First opened in 1919, this is the last remaining silk shop in town dedicated to selling Como-designed-and-made silk ties, scarves, throws and sarongs. Products are grouped in price category (starting at €10 for a tie), reflecting the skill and workmanship involved.

ℹ️ Information

Main Tourist Office (📞 031 26 97 12; www.comotourism.it; Piazza Cavour 17; ⏰9am-1pm & 2-5pm Mon-Sat) Como's main tourist office.

Tourist Office (📞 031 26 42 15; www.comotourism.it; Via Comacini; ⏰10.30am-5.30pm Mon-Fri, 10am-6pm Sat & Sun) Beside the *duomo*.

Tourist Office (📞 031 449 95 39; www.comotourism.it; Como San Giovanni, Piazzale San Gottardo; ⏰9am-5pm summer, 9.30pm-4.30pm Wed-Mon winter) Inside the San Giovanni train station.

Bellagio

POP 3090

Bellagio's waterfront of bobbing boats, its maze of steep stone staircases and its gardens filled with rhododendrons are a true joy. Inevitably these draw the summer crowds – stay overnight for a more authentic feel and the full magical effect.

⭕ Sights

⭐**Villa Serbelloni** GARDENS
(📞 031 95 15 55; Piazza della Chiesa 14; adult/child €9/5; ⏰tours 11.30am & 2.30pm Tue-Sun mid-Mar–Oct) This villa has been a magnet for Europe's great and good, including Austria's emperor Maximilian I, Ludovico il Moro and Queen Victoria. The interior is closed to the public, but you can explore the terraced park and gardens by guided tour only. Numbers are limited; tickets are sold at the PromoBellagio (p75) information office near the church.

Villa Melzi d'Eril GARDENS
(📞 339 4573838; www.giardinidivillamelzi.it; Lungo Lario Manzoni; adult/reduced €6.50/4; ⏰9.30am-6.30pm Apr-Oct) The grounds of neoclassical Villa Melzi d'Eril are a highlight among Lago di Como's (many) delightful places. The villa was built in 1808 for one of Napoleon's associates and is coloured by flowering azaleas and rhododendrons in spring. The statue-studded gardens was the first English-style park on the lake.

🏃 Activities

Lido SWIMMING
(📞 031 95 11 95; www.lidodibellagio.com; Via Carcano 1; per half/full day €8/12; ⏰10.30am-6.30pm Tue-Sun May, Jun & Sep, daily to 7.30pm Jul & Aug) With its sand-covered decking, diving platforms and gazebos, Bellagio's *lido* is a prime place to laze on a sun lounger or plunge into the lake.

Bellagio Water Sports KAYAKING
(📞 340 3949375; www.bellagiowatersports.com; Pescallo Harbour; rental per 2/4hr €18/30, tours €35) Sit-on-top kayak rental and two-hour tours taking in some of Como's most photogenic sites are possible from this experienced outfit in Pescallo, on the east side of the Bellagio headland.

🍴 Courses

⭐**Bellagio Cooking Classes** COOKING COURSE
(📞 333 7860090; www.gustoitalianobellagio.com; Salita Plinio 5; per person €65-80) A wonderful way to really get to know Bellagio, these cooking classes have a personal touch – they take you to the village shops to buy the food and then local home cooks lead the sessions. Classes are small (a minimum of two, maximum of five).

🛏️ Sleeping

Locanda Barchetta B&B €
(📞 031 95 10 30; www.ristorantebarchetta.com; Via Centrale 13; d €95; 🛜) A great-value, central hideaway tucked into Bellagio's maze of cobbled streets. Barchetta provides small, unfussy but spruce rooms and a fabulous breakfast.

⭐**Hotel Silvio** HOTEL €€
(📞 031 95 03 22; www.bellagiosilvio.com; Via Carcano 10; d €135-185, meals €30-40; 🅿❄🛜🏊) Located above the fishing hamlet of Loppia a short walk from the village, this family-run hotel is one of Bellagio's best. Here you can wake up in a contemporary Zen-like room and gaze out over the gardens of some of Lago di Como's most prestigious villas. Then spend the morning at Bellagio's *lido;* it's free for hotel guests.

🍽️ Eating & Drinking

⭐**Ittiturismo da Abate** SEAFOOD €€
(📞 031 91 49 86; www.ittiturismodabate.it; Frazione Villa 4, Lezzeno; meals €25-35; ⏰7-10.30pm Tue-Sun, noon-2.30pm Sun; 🅿🚸) Most dishes at Slow Food–focused Da Abate feature fish that's been caught that day in the lake (the restaurant will only open if they've caught enough), so you can sample *lavarello* in balsamic vinegar, linguine with perch and black olives, and the robust *missoltino* (fish dried in salt and bay leaves). Da Abate is 8km south of Bellagio. Bookings advised.

Terrazza Barchetta ITALIAN €€
(📞 031 95 13 89; www.ristorantebarchetta.com; Salita Mella 13; pizza €10, meals €40-45; ⏰noon-

2.30pm & 7-10.30pm) The intimate terrace just above a crossroads of laneways in Bellagio's old town is a fine place for a meal. The restaurant has been around since 1887, which is plenty of time to perfect dishes such as deboned white lake fish in a pistachio crust or guinea fowl with whisky and mushroom sauce.

Bar Rossi
CAFE, BAR

(☑031 95 01 96; Piazza Mazzini 22; snacks €3-8; ☻7.30am-midnight Apr-Sep, to 10.30pm Oct-Mar) All gleaming walnut wood, glinting mirrors and regiments of bottles, the art nouveau Bar Rossi is one cafe not to miss. Revel in the elegant interior or take a seat outside under the arches and watch the ferries come and go.

🛍 Shopping

Caligari Alimentaria
FOOD

(Via Bellosio 1; ☻8.15am-1pm & 4-7pm Tue-Sat) The smells wafting out from this deli will surely tempt you to step inside. Among the piled-high Larian goodies are dried porcini mushrooms (€7.50 per 50g), DOP Laghi Lombardi-Lario olive oil and *missoltini*.

ℹ Information

PromoBellagio (☑031 95 15 55; www.bellagio lakecomo.com; Piazza della Chiesa 14; ☻9.30am-1pm Mon, 9-11am & 1.30-3.30pm Tue-Sun Apr-Oct) A consortium of local businesses that provides useful information.

Tourist Office (☑031 95 02 04; prombell@ tin.it; Piazza Mazzini; ☻9am-12.30pm & 1-6pm Mon-Sat, 10am-2pm Sun summer, reduced hours winter) The official tourist office, next to the boat landing stage. Can provide information on water sports, mountain biking and other activities.

Cernobbio to Lenno

The sunny, western lake-front stretch from Cernobbio to Lenno is one of Lago di Como's most glamorous. The big draws here are the blockbuster villas; some are open to the public (such as the bewitching Villa Balbianello); some are most definitely closed (including George Clooney's place, Villa Oleandra, in Laglio).

👁 Sights

★ Villa Balbianello
VILLA, GARDENS

(☑0344 5 61 10; www.fondoambiente.it; Via Comoedia 5, Località Balbianello; villa & gardens adult/reduced €15/7, gardens only €8/3; ☻gardens 10am-6pm Tue & Thu-Sun mid-Mar–mid-Nov) A 1km walk along the lake shore from Lenno's main square, Villa Balbianello has cinematic pedigree: this was where scenes from *Star Wars Episode II* and the 2006 James Bond remake of *Casino Royale* were shot. The reason? It is one of the most dramatic locations anywhere on Lago di Como, providing a genuinely stunning marriage of architecture and lake views.

Visitors are only allowed to walk the 1km path (amid vegetation so florid as to seem Southeast Asian) from the Lenno landing stage to the estate on Tuesdays and at weekends. On other days, you have to take a taxi boat (☑349 2290952; www. taxiboatlecco.com; return €7) from Lenno. If you want to see inside the villa, you must join a guided tour (generally conducted in Italian) by 4.15pm.

Tremezzo

POP 1240

Tremezzo draws fleets of ferries thanks to its 17th-century Villa Carlotta and spectacular Lago di Como views.

👁 Sights

Villa Carlotta
VILLA, GARDENS

See p24.

🛏 Sleeping & Eating

★ Hotel La Perla
HOTEL €€

(☑0344 4 17 07; www.laperlatremezzo.com; Via Romolo Quaglino 7; d €125-145, with lake views €140-165, family ste €185-235; P❄☎☺) It's rare that hotels are so universally acclaimed as this one. Rooms are immaculate, service is warm and friendly and the vantage point from the hillside setting is one of Lago di Como's loveliest. All this is housed in an artful reconstruction of a 1960s villa. It's worth paying extra for a room with a view.

Al Veluu
RISTORANTE €€€

(☑0344 4 05 10; www.alveluu.com; Via Rogaro 11; meals €40-70; ☻noon-2.30pm & 7-10pm Wed-Mon; 🅟) Situated on a steep hillside with panoramic lake views from its terrace, this excellent restaurant serves up home-cooked dishes that are prepared with great pride. They also reflect Lago di Como's seasonal produce, so expect butter-soft, milk-fed kid with rosemary at Easter or wild asparagus and polenta in spring.

Varenna streetscape

ℹ Information

Tremezzo Tourist Office (☎0344 4 04 93;
Via Statale Regina; ☺9am-noon & 3.30-
6.30pm Wed-Mon Apr-Oct) By the boat jetty.

Varenna

Varenna clings to Lago di Como's shadier,
wilder eastern shore, vying for the title
of prettiest village on the lake. Its pastel-
coloured houses rise steeply up the hillside; a series of lanes and stairways slither
down to the water's edge.

◉ Sights

Villa Cipressi   GARDENS
(☎0341 83 01 13; www.hotelvillacipressi.it; Via
IV Novembre 22; adult/child €4/2; ☺10am-
6pm Mar-Oct) In Villa Cipressi's gardens,
cypress trees, palms, magnolias and camellias fill terraces that descend to the
lake. Even getting here is picturesque:
from the square next to the boat jetty (Piazzale Martiri della Libertà), follow the
narrow lakeside promenade around the
shore then bear left (inland) up the steps
to central Piazza San Giorgio. The villa is
signposted from there.

Villa Monastero   VILLA, GARDENS
See p24.

🛏 Sleeping

Albergo Milano   HOTEL €€
(☎0341 83 02 98; www.varenna.net; Via XX
Settembre 35; s €125, d €150-190; ☺Mar-Oct;
❋@☎) In the middle of Varenna on the
pedestrian main street (well, lane), hillside Albergo Milano opens onto a terrace
with magnificent lake vistas. Most of the
12 rooms have some kind of lake view and
balcony – they're also tastefully appointed,
with gaily painted iron bedsteads, dark-
wood wardrobes and creamy-white linen.

✖ Eating & Drinking

★**Vecchia Varenna**   ITALIAN €€
(☎0341 83 07 93; www.vecchiavarenna.it; Con-
trada Scoscesa 14; meals €35-45; ☺12.30-2pm
& 7.30-9.30pm Tue-Sun) You can't get more
lakeside than these 15 or so tables set on a
terrace suspended over the water. Which
means you can dine on lake fish, duck
breast or little gnocchi cooked in goat's
cheese, cream and truffle oil while gazing
over towards Como's western shore.

Il Molo   BAR
(☎0341 83 00 70; www.barilmolo.it; Via Riva
Garibaldi 14; ☺11am-1am Apr-Oct) The tiny
terrace of Bar Il Molo is Varenna's most
sought-after *aperitivi* spot. It's raised
above the water with cracking views
north right up the lake.

ℹ Information

Tourist Office (☎0341 81 40 09; www.
varennaitaly.com; Via Per Esino 3; ☺9.30am-
12.30pm & 2-6.30pm Tue-Sat, 9.30am-
12.30pm Sun Jul, shorter hours rest of year)
Varenna's tourist office can provide information on the lake's entire eastern shore.

Lago di Garda

Poets and politicians, divas and dictators,
they've all been drawn to Lago di Garda. At
370 sq km it is the largest of the Italian lakes,
straddling the border between Lombardy
and the Veneto, with soaring mountains
to the north and softer hills to the south.
Everywhere villages line a string of natural
harbours, and vineyards, olive groves and
citrus trees range up the slopes.

ℹ️ Information

The website www.visitgarda.com is a good source of lake-wide information.

Sirmione

POP 8010

Sitting on an impossibly narrow peninsula on the southern shore, Sirmione is often proclaimed Largo di Garda's most picturesque village. Throughout the centuries it has attracted notables from the Roman poet Catullus to Maria Callas, and today thousands continue to follow in their footsteps.

🔘 Sights & Activities

Rocca Scaligera　　　　　　　　CASTLE
(Castello Scaligero; ☑030 91 64 68; adult/reduced €4/2; ⊙8.30am-7pm Tue-Sat, to 1.30pm Sun) Expanding their influence northwards, the Scaligeri of Verona built this enormous square-cut castle right at the entrance to Sirmione. It guards the only footbridge into town, and looms over it with impressive crenellated turrets and towers. There's not a lot inside, but the climb up 146 steps to the top of the tower affords beautiful views over Sirmione's rooftops and the enclosed harbour.

★Grotte di Catullo　　ARCHAEOLOGICAL SITE
See p30.

★Aquaria　　　　　　　　　　　SPA
(☑030 91 60 44; www.termedisirmione.com; Piazza Piatti; pools per hour/day €15/53, treatments from €30; ⊙pools 10am-10pm Sun-Wed & Fri, to midnight Thu & Sat Mar-Dec, hours vary Jan & Feb) Sirmione is blessed with a series of offshore thermal springs that pump out water at a natural 37°C. They were discovered in the late 1800s and the town's been tapping into their healing properties ever since. At the Aquaria spa you can wallow in two thermal pools – the outdoor one is set right beside the lake.

🍴 Sleeping & Eating

Many of Sirmione's hotels close from the end of October through to March. Four campgrounds lie near the town; the tourist office can advise.

★Grifone　　　　　　　　　　HOTEL €
(☑030 91 60 14; www.gardalakegrifonehotel.eu; Via Gaetano Bocchio 4; s €65-75, d €85-115, tr €125-140) The location is superb: set right beside the shore, Grifone's many bedrooms directly overlook the lake and Sirmione's castle. With this family-run hotel you get five-star views for two-star prices. Inside it's all old-school simplicity, but very spic and span.

Hotel Marconi　　　　　　　　HOTEL €€
(☑030 91 60 07; www.hotelmarconi.net; Via Vittorio Emanuele II 51; s €45-75, d €80-135; 🅿❄🛜) Blue-and-white-striped umbrellas line the lakeside deck at this stylish, family-run hotel. The quietly elegant light-filled rooms, some with balconies and lake views, sport subtle shades and crisp fabrics, while the breakfasts and homemade pastries are a treat.

La Fiasca　　　　　　　　　TRATTORIA €€
(☑030 990 61 11; www.trattorialafiasca.it; Via Santa Maria Maggiore; meals €30; ⊙noon-2.30pm & 7-10.30pm Thu-Tue) In this authentic trattoria, tucked away in a backstreet just off the main square, the atmosphere is warm and bustling, and the dishes are packed with traditional Lago di Garda produce. Prepare for some gutsy flavours: *bigoli* (thick spaghetti) with sardines, fillets of perch with asparagus, and duck with cognac and juniper.

ℹ️ Information

Tourist Office (☑030 91 61 14; iat.sirmione@ provincia.brescia.it; Viale Marconi 8; ⊙9am-12.30pm & 3-6pm, closed Sat afternoon & Sun winter) On the main road into Sirmione, just before the castle.

Salò

POP 10,600

Wedged between the lake and precipitous mountains, Salò exudes an air of grandeur. Its long waterfront promenade is lined with ornate buildings and palm trees, while the graceful bell tower of its 15th-century cathedral overlooks picturesque lanes.

🔘 Sights

★Isola del Garda　　　　ISLAND, GARDENS
(☑328 6126943; www.isoladelgarda.com; tour incl boat ride €25-30; ⊙Apr-Oct) It's not often you get to explore such a stunning private island, villa and grounds. Anchored just off Salò, this speck of land is crowned with impressive battlements, luxuriant formal gardens and a sumptuous neo-Gothic Venetian villa. Boats depart from towns including Salò, San Felice del Benaco, Gardone Riviera and Sirmione, but they only leave each location one or two times a week, so plan ahead.

The island is owned by the aristocratic Cavazza family; you may well see some of them strolling around. The tour price includes a small *aperitivo*.

Republic of Salò
AREA

In 1943 Salò was named the capital of the Social Republic of Italy as part of Mussolini and Hitler's last efforts to organise Italian Fascism in the face of advancing American forces. This episode, known as the Republic of Salò, saw more than 16 public and private buildings in the town commandeered and turned into Mussolini's ministries and offices. Strolling between the sites is a surreal tour of the dictator's doomed mini-state. Look out for the multilingual plaques scattered around town.

🛏 Sleeping

⭐**Aromi**   BOUTIQUE HOTEL **€€**
(📞0365 2 20 49; www.aromipiccolohotel.com; Via Calsone 34; s €75-100, d €95-120; @🛜) With its ultracool lines, oatmeal-and-cream colour scheme and supersleek bathrooms, the town-centre Aromi is irresistible. It is set beside a main road, but the swish design and breakfasts piled high with pastries and fruit more than compensate. The same outfit runs three smart two-to-four person apartments (€80 to €155) in the pedestrianised old town nearby.

Gardone Riviera

POP 270

Gardone's glory days were in the late 19th and early 20th centuries, and today the resort's opulent villas and ornate architecture make it one of Lago di Garda's most elegant holiday spots.

About 12km north of Gardone lies Gargnano, a tiny harbour that fills with million-dollar yachts come September when sailing fans gather for the Centomiglia, the lake's most prestigious sailing regatta.

⊙ Sights

⭐**Il Vittoriale degli Italiani**   MUSEUM
(📞0365 29 65 11; www.vittoriale.it; Piazza Vittoriale; gardens & museums adult/reduced €16/12; ⊙grounds 8.30am-8pm Apr-Sep, to 5pm Oct-Mar, museums 8.30am-6.30pm Tue-Sun Apr-Sep, 9am-1pm & 2-5pm Tue-Sun Oct-Mar) Visit this estate and you'll take in a dimly lit, highly idiosyncratic villa, a war museum and tiered gardens complete with full-sized battleship.

In the main house of proto-Fascist poet Gabriele d'Annunzio (1863–1938), the Prioria, stained-glass windows cast an eerie light on gloomy rooms with black velvet drapes (he had an eye condition that made exposure to sunlight painful). The rooms are crammed with classical figurines, leather-bound books, leopard skins, gilded ornaments, lacquer boxes and chinoiserie. Highlights include the bronze tortoise that sits on the guests' dining table (in admonition of gluttony; it was cast from a pet that died of overindulgence); the bright blue bathroom suite with more than 2000 pieces of bric-a-brac; his spare bedroom where he would retire to lie on a coffin-shaped bed and contemplate death; and his study with its low lintel – designed so visitors would have to bow as they entered. Guided visits, in Italian only, tour the house every 15 minutes and last half an hour.

If you aren't already overwhelmed by d'Annunzio's excesses, the estate's Museo della Guerra is housed nearby in the art nouveau Casa Schifamondo (Escape from the World). It is full of mementoes, banners and medals of d'Annunzio's wartime exploits, while the gardens offer the chance to wander the deck of the full-sized battleship *Puglia,* which d'Annunzio used in his Fiume exploits.

⭐**Giardino Botanico Fondazione André Heller**   GARDENS, SCULPTURE
(📞336 41 08 77; www.hellergarden.com; Via Roma 2; adult/child €10/5; ⊙9am-7pm Mar-Oct) Gardone's heyday was due in large part to its mild climate, something which benefits the thousands of exotic blooms that fill André Heller's sculpture garden. Laid out in 1912 by Arturo Hruska, the garden is divided into pocket-sized climate zones, with tiny paths winding from central American plains to African savannah, via swathes of tulips and bamboo.

The playful touches hidden among the greenery include 30 pieces of contemporary sculpture – look out for the jagged red figure by Keith Haring near the entrance, Rudolf Hirt's Gaudi-esque *Ioanes, God of Water,* and Roy Lichtenstein's polka-dot take on the pyramids.

Sleeping & Eating

★**Locanda Agli Angeli** B&B €€
(☎0365 2 09 91; www.agliangeli.biz; Via Dosso 7; s €70, d €135-170; P❄≋) It's a perfect hillside Lago di Garda bolt-hole: a beautifully restored, rustic-chic *locanda* (inn) with a pint-sized pool and a terrace dotted with armchairs. Ask for room 29 for a balcony with grandstand lake and hill views, but even the smaller bedrooms are full of charm.

The restaurant (hours vary) is renowned for classic Lago di Garda dishes, or opt for supper in the inn's new nearby pizzeria, which comes with wide water views.

Information

Tourist Office (☎0365 374 87 36; Corso della Repubblica 8; ⏱9am-12.30pm & 2.15-6pm Mon-Sat) The tourist office stocks information on activities.

DON'T MISS

TASTING OLIVE OIL

Lake Garda's microclimate resembles the Mediterranean's, which ensures ideal olive-growing conditions. A tiny 1% of Italy's olive oil is produced here, but it's renowned for being light, soft and sweet.

The Comincioli family has been harvesting olives for nearly 500 years and produces some of Italy's best olive oils – the family's Numero Uno is legendary. Gain an insight into the complex process and indulge in a tutored tasting at their **farm-vineyard** (☎0365 65 11 41; www.comincioli.it; Via Roma 10, Puegnago del Garda; ⏱by reservation 9.30am-noon & 2.30-7pm Mon-Sat) FREE deep in the Valtenesi hills.

Riva del Garda & Around

POP 16,700

Even situated on a lake that is blessed with dramatic scenery, Riva del Garda comes out on top. Encircled by towering rock faces and a looping strip of beach, its appealing centre is a medley of elegant architecture, mazelike streets and wide squares.

Riva is in the Alpine region of Trentino-Alto Adige, but for centuries its strategic position saw it fought over by the Republic of Venice, Milan's Viscontis and Verona's Della Scala families, with the town remaining part of Austria until 1919.

Sights

★**Cascata del Varone** WATERFALL
(☎0464 52 14 21; www.cascata-varone.com; Via Cascata 12; admission €5.50; ⏱9am-7pm May-Aug, to 6pm Apr & Sep, to 5pm Mar & Oct) Prepare to get wet – this 100m waterfall cascades down sheer limestone cliffs through an immense, natural gorge. Spray-soaked walkways snake 50m into the mountain beside the crashing torrent, and strolling along them is like walking in a perpetual thunderstorm. You'll find it signposted 3km northwest of Riva's centre.

Museo Alto Garda MUSEUM
(La Rocca; ☎0464 57 38 69; www.museoaltogarda.it; Piazza Cesare Battisti 3; adult/reduced €3/1.50; ⏱10am-6pm Tue-Sun mid-Mar–May & Oct, daily Jun-Sep) Housed in Riva's compact medieval castle, the civic museum features local archaeology, frescoes from Roman Riva, documents and paintings. In light of Riva's much fought over past, perhaps the most revealing exhibits are the antique maps dating from 1579 and 1667, and a 1774 *Atlas Tyrolensis,* which evocatively convey the area's shifting boundaries.

Sleeping

★**Hotel Garni Villa Maria** HOTEL €
(☎0464 55 22 88; www.garnimaria.com; Viale dei Tigli; s €40-75, d €70-115, apt €100-340; P❄🛜👪) Beautifully designed, ubermodern rooms make this small family-run hotel a superb deal. Pristine bedrooms have a Scandinavian vibe, with all-white linens, sleek modern bathrooms and accents of orange and lime green. There's a tiny roof garden, and bedrooms with balconies offer soaring mountain views.

Lido Palace HISTORIC HOTEL €€€
(☎0464 02 18 99; www.lido-palace.it; Viale Carducci 10; d €290-420, ste €450-755; P❄@🛜≋) If you're going to splash the cash, this is the place to do it. Riva's captivating Lido Palace dates back to 1899. Sensitive renovations mean modern bedrooms with muted colour schemes now sit in the grand Liberty-style villa, offering peerless views over lawns and lake.

✖ Eating

★ Cristallo Caffè — GELATERIA €
(☑ 0464 55 38 44; www.cristallogelateria.com; Piazza Catena 11; cones €2.50; ⊙ 7am-1am) More than 60 flavours of artisanal gelato are served up in this lakeside cafe, crafted by the Panciera family, which has been making gelato since 1892. It's also a top spot to sip a *spritz* (cocktail made with Prosecco) while enjoying water and lake views.

★ Restel de Fer — ITALIAN €€
(☑ 0464 55 34 81; www.resteldefer.com; Via Restel de Fer 10; meals €40-60; ⊙ noon-2.30pm & 7-11pm daily Jul & Aug, Thu-Tue Sep, Oct & Dec-Jun; P 🛜) Going to the restaurant at this family-run *locanda* feels like dropping by a friend's rustic-chic house: expect worn leather armchairs, copper cooking pots and glinting blue glass. The menu focuses on seasonal, local delicacies such as rabbit wrapped in smoked mountain ham, char with crayfish, and veal with Monte Baldo truffles.

Upstairs, swish farmhouse-style accommodation (single €70, double €90 to €120) is chock-full of old oak dressers and hand-woven rugs. It's 1km east of the centre of Riva.

★ Osteria Le Servite — OSTERIA €€
(☑ 0464 55 74 11; www.leservite.com; Via Passirone 68, Arco; meals €30-45; ⊙ 7-10.30pm Tue-Sun Apr-Sep, 7-10.30pm Wed-Sat Oct-Mar; P 🛒) Tucked away in Arco's wine-growing region, this elegant little *osteria* serves dishes that are so seasonal the menu changes weekly. You might be eating mimosa gnocchi, tender *salmerino* (Arctic char) or organic ravioli with *stracchino* cheese.

Each dish comes with a suggested wine. In summer you can sit on the patio and sip small-production DOC Trentino vintages.

❶ Information

Tourist Office (☑ 0464 55 44 44; www. gardatrentino.it; Largo Medaglie d'Oro; ⊙ 9am-7pm May-Sep, to 6pm Oct-Apr) Can advise on everything from climbing and paragliding to wine tasting and markets.

Bardolino

Prosperous Bardolino is a town in love with the grape, with an abundance of vineyards and wine cellars scattered across the hills to the east of town. It is also a big spa town and the springboard for the ancient walled village of Lazise. Come early October, the town's waterfront fills with food and wine stands, as well as musicians and dancers. Year-round, there's a weekly market on Thursdays. For a map of local producers on the **Bardolino Strada del Vino** (www.stradadelbardolino.com) visit the tourist office. Barodolina is also a big spa town and the springboard for the ancient walled village of Lazise.

◉ Sights & Activities

Museo del Vino — MUSEUM
(☑ 045 622 83 31; www.museodelvino.it; Via Costabella 9; ⊙ 9am-1pm & 2.30-7pm mid-Mar–Sep, hours vary Oct–mid-Mar) **FREE** The Museo del Vino is within the Zeni winery, and rarely has a museum smelled so good. Rich aromas surround displays of wicker grape baskets, cooper's tools, drying racks and immense wooden presses. Tastings of Zeni's red, white and rosé wines are free, or pay to sample pricier vintages, including barrel-aged Amarone.

Zeni Winery — WINERY
(☑ 045 721 00 22; www.zeni.it; Via Costabella 9; tours €5) Zeni has been crafting quality wines from Bardolino's morainic hills since 1870. Get an insight into that process with an hour-long winery tour that ends with a mini-tasting in the *cantina* (cellar). Reservations aren't necessary; tours run every Wednesday at 11am, from May to September.

Or book a place on the two-hour Dolceamaro Raisining tour (per two people €100), and taste four dry Valpolicella wines, along with tangy local cheese, mustard and Monte Baldo honey, rounded off with a sweet Recioto dessert wine and some chocolatey *tortellini di Valeggio*.

✖ Eating

★ Il Giardino delle Esperidi — OSTERIA €€
(☑ 045 621 04 77; Via Goffredo Mameli 1; meals €35-50; ⊙ 7-10pm Mon & Wed-Fri, noon-2.30pm & 7-10pm Sat & Sun) Bardolino's gourmets head for this intimate little o*steria* where sourcing local delicacies is a labour of love for its sommelier-owner. The intensely flavoured baked truffles with *parmigiano reggiano* (Parmesan) are legendary, and the highly seasonal menu may feature rarities such as goose salami or guinea fowl salad.

🍷 Drinking & Nightlife

La Bottega del Vino — WINE BAR
(☑ 348 604 18 00; Piazza Matteotti 46; snacks €5, glass of wine from €2.50; ⊙ 10.30am-2pm &

5-10pm Sun-Thu, to midnight Fri & Sat) To experience some authentic Bardolino atmosphere head to this no-nonsense bar in the centre of town. Inside, a stream of lively banter passes between locals and staff beside walls lined with bottles four deep.

❶ Information

Tourist Office (☑045 721 00 78; www.tourism.verona.it; Piazzale Aldo Moro 5; ⊙9am-noon & 3-6pm Mon-Sat, 10am-2pm Sun) Operates a hotel booking service and can advise on the surrounding wine region.

Bergamo

POP 118,700

Bergamo is one of northern Italy's most attractive, interesting cities, with a walled Città Alta (Upper Town) that incorporates an array of medieval, Renaissance and baroque architecture. Despite sitting at the foot of the pre-Alps, the city was ruled by Venice for 350 years (1428–1797) until Napoleon arrived.

A funicular runs to the Città Alta from the more modern Città Bassa (Lower Town). A different funicular runs from the Città Alta to the quaint quarter of San Vigilio, which offers some stunning views.

◉ Sights

Cafe-clad Piazza Vecchia (Old Square) lies at the heart of the Città Alta's tangle of medieval streets. Lined by elegant architecture, it was dubbed by Le Corbusier 'the most beautiful square in Europe'.

★**Torre del Campanone** TOWER
(☑035 24 71 16; Piazza Vecchia; adult/child €3/free; ⊙9.30am-6pm Tue-Fri, to 8pm Sat & Sun Apr-Oct, reduced hours winter) Bergamo's colossal, square-based Torre del Campanone soars 52m above the city. It still tolls a bell at 10pm, the legacy of the old curfew. Taking the lift to the top of the tower reveals sweeping views down onto the town, up to the pre-Alps and across to the Lombard plains.

★**Palazzo del Podestà** MUSEUM
(Museo Storico dell'Età Veneta; ☑035 24 71 16; www.palazzodelpodesta.it; Piazza Vecchia; adult/reduced €7/5; ⊙9.30am-1pm & 2.30-6pm Tue-Sun) In this superbly imaginative seven-room museum a rich range of audiovisual and interactive displays tell the story of Bergamo's Venetian age. Expect animated

Bergamo

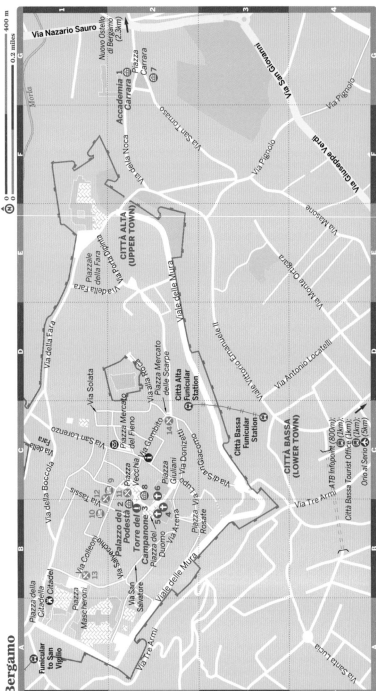

Via Nazario Sauro

Nuovo Ostello
di Bergamo (2.3km)

Morla

Via San Giovanni

Accademia 1
Carrara

Piazza
Carrara
7

Via della Noca

Via San Tomaso

Via Pignolo

Via Giuseppe Verdi

Via Pignolo

Piazzale
della Fara

Via Porta Dipinta

CITTÀ ALTA
(UPPER TOWN)

Via Masone

Via della Fara

Via della Fara

Viale delle Mura

Via Monte Ortigara

Via della Boccola

Via Solata

Piazza Mercato
del Fieno

Piazza Mercato
delle Scarpe

Città Alta
Funicular
Station

Viale Vittorio Emanuele II

Via Antonio Locatelli

Via della Fara

Via San Lorenzo

Via alla Rocca

14

Via Gombito

Città Bassa
Funicular
Station

CITTÀ BASSA
(LOWER TOWN)

Piazza Mercato
Vecchia

9

8

6

Piazza
Giuliani

Via Donizetti

Via di San Giacomo

Via Tassis

Palazzo del 2
Podestà 11

Torre del 1
Campanone 3

10

5
4

Piazza del
Duomo

Via Arena

Via Lupo

Piazza
Via Rosate

Via Tre Armi

Città Bassa Tourist Office (1km);

ATB Infopoint (800m);

(1km);

Orio al Serio (5km)

Via San Vecchio

Via Colleoni

13

Piazza della
Cittadella

Citadel

Piazza
Mascheroni

Via San Salvatore

Viale delle Mura

Funicular
to San
Vigilio

Via Tre Armi

Via Santa Lucia

Bergamo

maps, high-tech re-creations of printing typefaces and a mock-up shop with drawers full of snakes. It's all set in the medieval, fresco-dotted Palazzo del Podestà, the traditional home to Venice's representative in the town.

Palazzo della Ragione　　HISTORIC BUILDING
(Piazza Vecchia) The imposing arches and columns of the Palazzo della Ragione sit at the southern end of Piazza Vecchia. Built in the 12th century, it bears the lion of St Mark – a reminder of Venice's long reign here. The animal is actually an early-20th-century replica of the 15th-century original, which was torn down when Napoleon took over in 1797. Note the sun clock in the pavement beneath the arches and the curious Romanesque and Gothic animals and busts decorating the pillars.

Duomo　　CATHEDRAL
(☑035 21 02 23; Piazza del Duomo; ☉7.30-11.45am & 3-6.30pm) Roman remains were discovered during renovations of Bergamo's baroque cathedral. A rather squat building, it has a brilliant white facade. Among the relics in a side chapel is the one-time coffin of the beatified Pope John XXII.

Basilica di Santa Maria Maggiore　　BASILICA
(Piazza del Duomo; ☉9am-12.30pm & 2.30-6pm Apr-Oct, shorter hours Nov-Mar) Begun in 1137, the Basilica di Santa Maria Maggiore is quite a mishmash of styles. Influences seem to come from afar, with dual-colour banding (black and white, and rose and white) typical of Tuscany and an interesting *trompe l'œil* pattern on part of the facade.

Cappella Colleoni　　CHAPEL
See p26.

★ **Accademia Carrara**　　GALLERY
(☑035 23 43 96; www.lacarrara.it; Piazza Carrara 82; adult/reduced €10/8; ☉9am-7pm) Just east of the old city walls is one of Italy's great art repositories. Founded in 1780, it contains an exceptional range of Italian masters. Raphael's *San Sebastiano* is a highlight, and other artists represented include Botticelli, Canaletto, Mantegna and Titian.

The collection was started by local scholar Count Giacomo Carrara (1714–96) and has now swelled to 1800 paintings dating from the 15th to 19th centuries. Reopened after a seven-year renovation, the gallery's displays revolve around 28 rooms. Highlights include the sections on Giovanni Bellini, Florence and the major local artists Lorenzo Lotto and Giovanni Battista Moroni.

Galleria d'Arte Moderna e Contemporanea　　GALLERY
(GAMeC; ☑035 27 02 72; www.gamec.it; Via San Tomaso 53; ☉10am-1pm & 3-7pm Tue-Sun) FREE The modern works by Italian artists displayed here include pieces by Giacomo Balla, Giorgio Morandi, Giorgio de Chirico and Filippo de Pisis. A contribution from Vassily Kandinsky lends an international touch.

🛏 Sleeping

Albergo Il Sole　　HOTEL €
(☑035 21 82 38; www.ilsolebergamo.com; Via Colleoni 1; s/d/tr €65/85/110; 🅰) Bright rugs and throws bring bursts of the modern to this traditional, family-run *albergo* (hotel) in the heart of the Città Alta; exposed stone and picture windows add to the quaint feel. The best room is 107, where the balcony offers mountain glimpses and roof-top views.

Nuovo Ostello di Bergamo　　HOSTEL €
(☑035 36 17 24; www.ostellodibergamo.it; Via Ferraris 1, Monterosso; dm/s/d €20/35/50; 🅿@🅰) Bergamo's state-of-the-art HI hostel is about 4km north of the train station. Its 27 rooms offer views over Bergamo's old town centre. Take bus 6 from Largo Porta Nuova near the train station (get off at Leonardo da Vinci stop) or bus 3 for Ostello from the Città Alta.

★**Hotel Piazza Vecchia** HOTEL €€
(☏035 25 31 79; www.hotelpiazzavecchia.it; Via
Colleoni 3; d €100-300; ❋@☜) The perfect
Città Alta bolt-hole, this 13th-century town
house oozes atmosphere, from the honey-
coloured beams and exposed stone to the
tasteful art on the walls. Rooms have parquet floors and bathrooms that gleam with
chrome; the deluxe ones have a lounge and
a balcony with mountain views.

✕ Eating

The *bergamaschi* (people from Bergamo)
like their polenta, and have even named
a classic sweet after it: *polenta e osei* are
pudding-shaped cakes filled with jam and
cream, topped with icing and chocolate
birds. Bergamo's other famous dish is *ca-
sonsèi*, aka *casoncelli* (a kind of ravioli
stuffed with spicy sausage meat).

★**Il Fornaio** PIZZA, BAKERY €
(Via Bartolomeo Colleoni 1; pizza slices €1.10-2;
☺8am-8pm Mon-Sat, 7.30am-8pm Sun) Join the
crowds that mill around this local favourite
for coffee that packs a punch and pizza slices that drip with ingredients: spinach laced
with creamy mozzarella or gorgonzola studded with walnuts. Take it away or compete
for a table upstairs.

Polentone ITALIAN €
(☏348 804 60 21; Piazza Mercato delle Scarpe 1;
meals €12; ☺11.30am-3.30pm & 6-10pm Mon-Thu,
11.30am-1am Sat, to 10pm Sun) Styling itself
as Italy's first polenta takeaway, Polentone
serves up steaming bowls of polenta in the
sauce of your choice, including wild boar
and venison. Choose between *gialla* (simple, corn polenta) or *taragna* (with taleggio
cheese and butter).

★**Osteria della Birra** OSTERIA €€
(☏035 24 24 40; www.elavbrewery.com; Piazza
Mascheroni 1; meals €25-30; ☺noon-3pm & 6pm-
2am Mon-Fri, noon-2am Sat & Sun) Being the
official *osteria* of craft brewers, this convivial eatery ensures there's a top selection on
tap; the tangy Indie Ale tastes particularly
fine. So squeeze in at a tiny table or lounge
in the courtyard and chow down on platters
piled high with local meats, or polenta with
beef simmered in Elav's own-brewed beer.

★**Colleoni & Dell'Angelo** ITALIAN €€€
(☏035 23 25 96; www.colleonidellangelo.com; Piazza Vecchia 7; meals €50-60; ☺noon-2.30pm
& 7-10.30pm Tue-Sun) Grand Piazza Vecchia

provides the ideal backdrop to savour truly
top-class creative cuisine. Sit at an outside
table in summer or opt for the noble 15th-
century interior; either way expect to encoun-
ter dishes such as black risotto with ricotta
and grilled cuttlefish, or venison medallions
with chestnut purée and redcurrant jam.

❶ Information

Airport Tourist Office (☏035 32 04 02; www.
visitbergamo.net; arrivals hall; ☺8am-9pm)
Città Alta Tourist Office (☏035 24 22 26;
www.visitbergamo.net; Via Gombito 13; ☺9am-
5.30pm) In the heart of the Upper Town.
Città Bassa Tourist Office (☏035 21 02 04;
www.visitbergamo.net; Viale Papa Giovanni
XXIII 57; ☺9am-12.30pm & 2-5.30pm) Near the
train and bus stations, in the Lower Town.

Brescia

POP 193,600

Urban sprawl, a seedy bus and train station,
and the odd 1960s skyscraper don't hint at
Brescia's fascinating old town, which serves
as a reminder of its substantial history. Its
narrow streets are home to some of the
most important Roman ruins in Lombardy
and an extraordinary circular Romanesque
church.

◉ Sights

★**Santa Giulia** MUSEUM, MONASTERY
See p40.

Tempio Capitolino RUIN
(www.bresciamusei.com; Via dei Musei; adult/
reduced €4/3; ☺10am-5pm Tue-Sun Mar-Sep,
Fri-Sun Oct-Feb) Brescia's most impressive
Roman relic is this temple built by Emper-
or Vespasian in AD 73. Today six Corinthian
columns stand before a series of cells. Guided tours (50 minutes, hourly) reveal authentic decorations, including original coloured
marble floors, altars and religious statues.

Tickets also secure admission to Brescia's
nearby Roman Theatre.

Roman Theatre RUIN
(off Via dei Musei; adult/reduced €4/3; ☺10am-
5pm Fri-Sun) At the height of the Roman era,
the theatre of Brescia (then Brixia) could
seat 15,000 spectators. The surviving ruins
are now somewhat overgrown; find them at
the end of cobbled Vicolo del Fontanon.

Duomo Vecchio
CHURCH

(Old Cathedral; Piazza Paolo VI; ⊙9am-noon & 3-6pm Wed-Sat, 9-10.45am & 3-6pm Sun) The most compelling of all Brescia's religious monuments is the 11th-century Duomo Vecchio, a rare example of a circular-plan Romanesque basilica, built over a 6th-century church. The inside is surmounted by a dome borne by eight sturdy vaults resting on thick pillars.

Interesting features include fragmentary floor mosaics (perhaps from a thermal bath that might have stood here in the 1st century BC) and the elaborate 14th-century sarcophagus of Bishop Berado Maggi.

Museo Mille Miglia
MUSEUM

(☑030 336 56 31; www.museomillemiglia.it; Viale della Rimembranza 3; adult/reduced €7/5; ⊙10am-6pm) The original Mille Miglia (Thousand Miles) ran between 1927 and 1957 and was one of Italy's most legendary endurance car races – it started in Brescia and took some 16 hours to complete. The race's colourful museum is loaded with some of the greatest cars to cross the finish line, as well as old-style petrol pumps and archive race footage.

🍴 Sleeping & Eating

Risotto, beef dishes and *lumache alla Bresciana* (snails cooked with Parmesan cheese and fresh spinach) are common in Brescia.

★ Albergo Orologio
HOTEL €

(☑030 375 54 11; www.albergoorologio.it; Via Beccaria 17; s €64-85, d €84-94; 🕸@🛜) Just opposite from its namesake clock tower and just steps away from central Piazza Paolo VI, the medieval Albergo Orologio boasts fragrant rooms dotted with antiques. Bedrooms feature terracotta floors, soft gold, brown and olive furnishings, and snazzy modern bathrooms.

★ Osteria al Bianchi
OSTERIA €€

(☑030 29 23 28; www.osteriaalbianchi.it; Via Gasparo da Salò 32; meals €25; ⊙9am-2pm & 4.30pm-midnight Thu-Mon) Squeeze inside this classic bar, in business since 1880, or grab a pavement table and be tempted by the *pappardelle al taleggio e zucca* (broad ribbon pasta with taleggio cheese and pumpkin), followed by anything from *brasato d'asino* (braised donkey) to *pestöm* (minced pork served with polenta).

🍷 Drinking & Nightlife

Il Bottega
WINE BAR

(☑030 240 00 59; Via dei Musei 21; ⊙6pm-midnight Tue-Sun, to 1am Fri & Sat, noon-2pm Sat & Sun) A cool crowd crams into this buzzing bar to sip on classy wines and sample piled-high platters of meats and cheese (€4 to €7).

❶ Information

Main Tourist Office (☑030 240 03 57; www.turismobrescia.it; Via Trieste 1; ⊙9.30am-1pm & 1.30-5pm, to 6pm summer) Brescia's main tourist office, on the edge of Piazza Paolo VI, can advise on exploring the city's churches and Roman sites.

There's another, smaller tourist office at the **train station** (☑030 837 85 59; www.turismobrescia.it; Piazzale Stazione).

Mantua

POP 48,600

As serene as the three lakes it sits beside, Mantua is home to sumptuous ducal palaces and a string of atmospheric, cobbled squares. The city's heritage is rich: Latin poet Virgil was born here, Shakespeare had Romeo hear of Juliet's death here and Verdi set his tragic opera *Rigoletto* in these fog-bound streets. In 1328 the city fell to the fast-living, art-loving Gonzaga dynasty – their legacy lingers in the city today.

◉ Sights

The tight-knit centre of Mantua is like an alfresco medieval and Renaissance architectural museum, comprising from north to south: Piazza Sordello, Piazza Broletto, Piazza delle Erbe and Piazza Mantegna.

★ Palazzo Ducale
PALACE

(☑041 241 18 97; www.ducalemantova.org; Piazza Sordello 40; adult/reduced €13/8; ⊙8.15am-7.15pm Tue-Sun) For more than 300 years the enormous Palazzo Ducale was the seat of the Gonzaga – a family of wealthy horse breeders who rose to power in the 14th century to become one of Italy's leading Renaissance families. Their 500-room palace is vast; a visit today winds through 40 of the finest chambers. Along with works by Morone and Rubens, the highlight is the witty mid-15th-century fresco by Mantegna in the Camera degli Sposi (Bridal Chamber).

Mantua

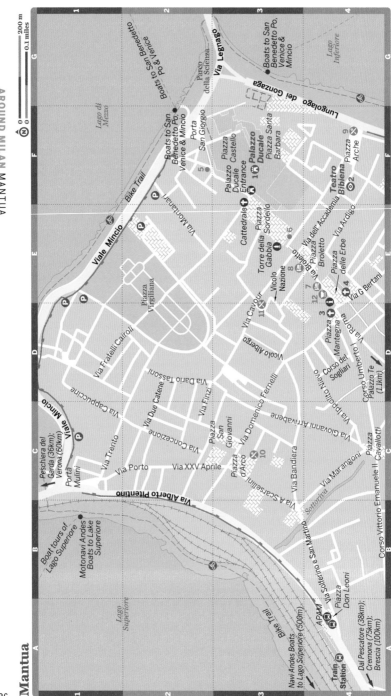

0 ———— 200 m
0 ———— 0.1 miles

Mantua

Rotonda di San Lorenzo CHURCH
(☏0376 32 22 97; Piazza delle Erbe; ⊙10am-1pm &
3-6pm Mon-Fri, 10am-6pm Sat & Sun) The weather-
worn 11th-century Rotonda di San Lorenzo
is sunk below the level of the square, its red-
brick walls still decorated with the shadowy
remains of 12th- and 13th-century frescoes.

Basilica di Sant'Andrea BASILICA
(☏0376 32 85 04; Piazza Mantegna; ⊙8am-noon
& 3-7pm) This towering basilica safeguards
the golden vessels said to hold earth soaked
by the blood of Christ. Longinus, the Roman
soldier who speared Christ on the cross, is
said to have scooped up the earth and buried
it in Mantua after leaving Palestine. Today,
these containers rest beneath a marble oc-
tagon in front of the altar and are paraded
around Mantua in a grand procession on
Good Friday.

★Teatro Bibiena THEATRE
(Teatro Scientifico; ☏0376 32 76 53; www.societa
dellamusica.it; Via dell'Accademia 47; adult/reduced
€2/1.20; ⊙10am-1pm & 3-4pm Tue-Fri, 10am-6pm
Sat & Sun) If ever a theatre were set to up-
stage the actors, it's the 18th-century Teatro
Bibiena. Dimly lit and festooned with plush
velvet, its highly unusual, intimate bell-
shaped design sees four storeys of ornate,
stucco balconies arranged around curving
walls. It was specifically intended to allow
its patrons to be seen – balconies even fill
the wall behind the stage.

Palazzo Te PALACE
(☏0376 32 32 66; www.palazzote.it; Viale Te 13;
adult/reduced €12/9; ⊙1-6pm Mon, 9am-6pm
Tue-Sun) Palazzo Te was where Frederico II
Gonzaga escaped for love trysts with his
mistress Isabella Boschetti. A Renaissance
pleasure-dome, it is the finest work of star
architect Giulio Romano, whose sumptuous
Mannerist scheme fills the palace with fanciful flights of imagination.

◎ Tours

Boat Tours BOAT TOUR
Short one- to two-hour tours on the lakes
that surround Mantua are offered by two
competitor companies, **Motonavi Andes**
(☏0376 32 28 75; www.motonaviandes.it; Via
San Giorgio 2) and **Navi Andes** (☏0376 32
45 06; www.naviandes.com; Piazza Sordello 48),
between April and October. Trips start at
around €9 and skirt lotus flowers, reed beds
and heron roosts, providing romantic city
views. Both companies also occasionally offer longer trips to Venice (one way €81) and
San Benedetto Po (adult/child €15.50/14.50)
through Parco del Mincio. These trips leave
from jetties either on Viale Mincio or Lun-
golago dei Gonzaga.

★Visit Mantua WALKING TOUR
(☏347 4022020; www.visitmantua.it; tours per 2
people 90min/5hr €100/300) Get the insider
view of Renaissance dukes and duchesses –
what they ate for breakfast, how they con-
spired at court and the wardrobe crises of
the day – with Lorenzo Bonoldi's fascinating
conversational tours of Mantua's palaces.

◎ Sleeping

Casa Margherita B&B €
(☏349 7506117; www.lacasadimargherita.it; Via
Broletto 44; s €60-65, d €80-100; ❋) For a
budget sleep, it's hard to top this elegant
town house, set in the heart of historic
Mantua. Artfully lit bedrooms combine soft
tones with subtle furnishings; bathrooms
team mod-cons with retro designs. Some
rooms have views onto Piazza Broletto.

★C'a delle Erbe B&B €€
(☏0376 22 61 61; www.cadelleerbe.it; Via Broletto 24; d €120-140; ❋🛜) In this exquisite
16th-century town house historic features
have had a minimalist makeover: exposed
stone walls surround paired-down furniture; white-painted beams coexist with
lavish bathrooms and modern art. The pick

of the bedrooms? The one with the balcony overlooking the iconic Piazza delle Erbe.

✖ Eating & Drinking

Mantua's most famous dish is melt-in-your-mouth *tortelli di zucca* (pumpkin-stuffed pasta). Look out too for *salumi* (salt pork), *prosciutto crudo* (salt-cured ham) and the sweet mustards *mostarda di mele* and *mantovana* (made with apples or pears).

Osteria delle Quattro Tette   OSTERIA €
(📞 0376 32 94 78; Vicolo Nazione 4; meals €10-15; ⏱ 12.30-2.30pm Mon-Sat) Take a pew at rough-hewn wooden tables beneath barrel-vaulted ceilings and order up pumpkin pancakes, pike in sweet salsa or *risotto alla pilota* (risotto with spiced sausage). It's spartan, rustic and extremely well priced, which is why half of Mantua is in here at lunchtime.

Fragoletta   MANTUAN €€
(📞 0376 32 33 00; www.fragoletta.it; Piazza Arche 5; meals €30; ⏱ noon-3pm & 8-11pm Tue-Sun; 🖤) Wooden chairs scrape against the tiled floor as diners eagerly tuck into Slow Food–accredited *culatello di Zibello* (lard) at this friendly local trattoria. Other Mantuan specialities feature, such as *risotto alla pilota* (rice studded with sausage meat) and pumpkin ravioli with melted butter and sage.

★ Il Cigno   MODERN ITALIAN €€€
(📞 0376 32 71 01; www.ristoranteilcignomantova.com; Piazza d'Arco 1; meals €55-65; ⏱ 12.30-2.30pm & 7-11pm Wed-Sun, closed part of Aug) The building is as beautiful as the food: a lemon-yellow facade dotted with faded olive-green shutters. Inside, Mantua's gourmets graze on delicately steamed risotto with spring greens, poached cod with polenta or gamey guinea fowl with spicy *mostarda*.

Bar Caravatti   CAFE, BAR
(📞 0376 32 78 26; Portici Broletto 16; ⏱ 7am-8.30pm) All of Mantua passes through Caravatti at some point during the day for coffee, *spritz* or Signor Caravatti's 19th-century *aperitivo* of aromatic bitters and wine.

ℹ Information

Tourist Office (📞 0376 43 24 32; www.turismo.mantova.it; Piazza Mantegna 6; ⏱ 9am-1.30pm & 2.30-6pm Tue-Fri, to 5pm Mon, 9am-6pm Sat & Sun)

Cremona

POP 71,200

A wealthy, independent city-state for centuries, Cremona boasts some fine medieval architecture, but is best known internationally for making the world's best violins.

◉ Sights

Piazza del Comune   PIAZZA
This beautiful, pedestrian-only piazza is considered one of the best-preserved medieval squares in all Italy. To maintain divisions between Church and state, Church buildings were erected on the eastern side and those for secular affairs were built on the west.

Duomo   CATHEDRAL
(Piazza del Comune; ⏱ 8am-noon & 2.30-6pm Mon-Sat, noon-12.30pm & 3.30-6pm Sun) Cremona's cathedral started out as a Romanesque basilica, but the simplicity of that style later gave way to an extravagance of designs. The interior frescoes are utterly overwhelming, with the *Storie di Cristo* (Stories of Christ) by Pordenone perhaps the highlights. One of the chapels contains what is said to be a thorn from Jesus' crown of thorns.

Torrazzo   TOWER
(Piazza del Comune; adult/reduced €5/4; ⏱ 10am-1pm & 2.30-6pm, closed Mon winter) Cremona's 111m-tall *torrazzo* (bell tower, although '*torrazzo*' translates literally as 'great, fat tower') soars above the city's central square. A total of 502 steps wind up to marvelous views across the city.

Chiesa di Sant'Agostino   CHURCH
(Piazza Sant'Agostino; ⏱ 8am-noon & 2.30-6pm Mon-Sat, noon-12.30pm & 3.30-6pm Sun) Once inside the Chiesa di Sant'Agostino, head for the third chapel on the right, the **Cappella Cavalcabò**, which features a stunning late-Gothic fresco cycle by Bonifacio Bembo and his assistants. One of the altars is graced with a 1494 painting by Pietro Perugino, *Madonna in trono e santi* (The Madonna Enthroned with Saints).

★彡 Festivals & Events

Festival di Cremona Claudio Monteverdi   MUSIC
(www.teatroponchielli.it; ⏱ May) A month-long series of concerts centred on Monteverdi

CREMONA'S VIOLINS

It was in Cremona, in the 17th century, that master craftsman Antonio Stradivari lovingly put together his first violins. His legacy continues today, in the 100 violin-making workshops clustered around Piazza del Comune. The Stradivarius violin is typically made from spruce (the top of the violin), willow (the internal blocks and linings) and maple (the back, ribs and neck), and is prized for its unique sound.

Cremona's state-of-the-art **Museo del Violino** (☑0372 08 08 09; www.museodelviolino.org; Piazza Marconi 5; adult/reduced €10/7; ☉10am-6pm Tue-Sun) brings together the city's historic violin collections, presenting them alongside the tools of the trade. It also houses a special room containing the drawings, moulds and tools Stradivari used in his workshop. To hear Cremona's violins in action, head to the 19th-century **Teatro Amilcare Ponchielli** (☑0372 02 20 01; www.teatroponchielli.it; Corso Vittorio Emanuele II 52); its season runs from October to June.

and other baroque-era composers, held in the Teatro Amilcare Ponchielli.

Stradivari Festival   MUSIC
(www.museodelviolino.org; ☉mid-Sep–mid-Oct) Focusing on music for string instruments. Held between mid-September and mid-October, it's organised by the Museo del Violino.

🛏 Sleeping

Albergo Duomo   HOTEL €
(☑0372 3 52 42; www.hotelduomocremona.com; Via Gonfalonieri 13; s/d/tr €60/80/100; P❋☎) Despite being embedded in the heart of the old town, this is a sleek, modern affair, with chocolate-brown and cream decor, smart

bathrooms, music-themed prints and views over a jumble of historic roofs.

L'Archetto   HOSTEL €
(☑0372 80 77 55; www.ostellocremona.com; Via Brescia 9; dm/s/d €27/30/58; ❋@☎) Cost-conscious musicians love this central, positively luxurious hostel where cheerful, modern bedrooms and three-bed dorms are pristine and thoughtfully furnished. Sadly, the limited reception hours (8am to 10am and 5pm to 9pm) – and no option to leave luggage – might be inconvenient.

Delliarti Design Hotel   DESIGN HOTEL €€
(☑0372 2 31 31; www.hoteldellearti.com; Via Bonomelli 8; s/d from €100/130; ❋☎) A firm favourite with visiting fashionistas, Cremona's hippest hotel is a high-tech vision of glass, concrete and steel. Stylish bedrooms feature clean lines, bold colours and artistic lighting. There are also some fun flourishes: undulating gold, corrugated corridors, and a bowl of liquorice allsorts on the front desk.

🍴 Eating

★**Hosteria 700**   CREMONESE €€
(☑0372 3 61 75; www.hosteria700.it; Piazza Gallina 1; meals €30-35; ☉noon-3pm Wed-Mon, 7.30-10pm Wed-Sun) Behind the dilapidated facade lurks a sparkling gem. Some of the vaulted rooms come with ceiling frescoes and the hearty Lombard cuisine comes at a refreshingly competitive cost.

La Sosta   OSTERIA €€
(☑0372 45 66 56; www.osterialasosta.it; Via Sicardo 9; meals €35-40; ☉12.15-2pm Tue-Sun, 7.15-10pm Tue-Sat) La Sosta is surrounded by violin-makers' workshops and is a suitably harmonious place to feast on regional delicacies such as *tortelli di zucca* (pumpkin pasta parcels) and baked snails.

ℹ Information

Tourist Office (☑0372 40 63 91; www.turismocremona.it; Piazza del Comune 5; ☉9.30am-1pm & 2-5pm)

Venice really needs no introduction. This incomparable union of art, architecture and life has been a fabled destination for centuries. Most of the world's most famous writers and artists have visited to admire the mosaics of San Marco, the Old Masters in the Accademia and the city's maze of calle (lanes) and canals.

Venice & Padua

VENICE

POP 59,000

Imagine the audacity of deciding to build a city on a lagoon. Instead of surrendering to the *acque alte* (high tide) like reasonable folk might do, Venetians flooded the world with vivid paintings, baroque music, modern opera, spice-route cuisine, bohemian-chic fashions and a Grand Canal's worth of *spritz*, the city's signature *prosecco* and Aperol cocktail.

Today cutting-edge architects and billionaire benefactors are spicing up the art scene, musicians are rocking out 18th-century instruments and backstreet *osterie* (taverns) are winning a Slow Food following.

Like a cat with nine lives, Venice has miraculously survived over 1200 years of war, plague and invasion, but it now faces its greatest threat: rising sea levels. This remains the biggest challenge facing the city, with rises predicted between 14cm and 80cm by 2100.

⊙ Sights

★**Basilica di San Marco**　　　BASILICA
See p43.

★**Palazzo Ducale**　　　MUSEUM
See p43.

Campanile　　　TOWER
(Bell Tower; Map p92; www.basilicasanmarco.it; Piazza San Marco; admission €8; ⊙9am-9pm summer, to 7pm spring & autumn, 9.30am-3.45pm winter; ⓈSan Marco) The basilica's 99m-tall bell tower has been rebuilt twice since its initial construction in AD 888. Galileo Galilei tested his telescope here in 1609, but modern-day visitors head to the top for 360-degree lagoon views and close encounters with the Marangona, the booming bronze bell that originally signalled the start and end of the working day for the craftsmen (*marangoni*) at the Arsenale shipyards. Today it rings twice a day: at noon and midnight.

Teatro La Fenice　　　THEATRE
(Map p92; ☑041 78 66 75; www.teatrolafenice. it; Campo San Fantin 1965; theatre visits adult/reduced €9/6.50, opera tickets from €66; ⊙tours 9.30am-6pm; ⓈSanta Maria del Giglio) Once its dominion over the high seas ended, Venice discovered the power of high Cs, hiring as San Marco choirmaster Claudio Monteverdi and opening La Fenice ('The Phoenix') in 1792. Rossini and Bellini staged operas here, Verdi premiered *Rigoletto* and *La Traviata*, and international greats Stravinsky, Prokofiev and Britten composed for the house, making La Fenice the envy of Europe. From January to July and September to October, opera season is in full swing. Tours are also possible with advance booking.

★**Palazzo Grassi**　　　MUSEUM
(Map p92; ☑box office 199 13 91 39, 041 523 16 80; www.palazzograssi.it; Campo San Samuele 3231; adult/reduced €15/10, 72hr ticket incl Punta della Dogana €20/15; ⊙10am-7pm Wed-Mon mid-Apr-Nov;

San Samuele) Grand Canal gondola riders gasp at first glimpse of massive sculptures by contemporary artists like Thomas Houseago docked in front of Giorgio Masari's 1749 neo-classical palace. French billionaire François Pinault's provocative art collection overflows Palazzo Grassi, while clever curation and art-star namedropping are the hallmarks of rotating temporary exhibits. Still, despite the artistic glamour, Tadao Ando's creatively repurposed interior architecture steals the show.

★ Gallerie dell'Accademia — GALLERY
See p43.

★ Peggy Guggenheim Collection — MUSEUM
(Map p92; ☑ 041 240 54 11; www.guggenheim-venice.it; Palazzo Venier dei Leoni 704; adult/reduced €15/9; ☉ 10am-6pm Wed-Mon; ⛴ Accademia) After losing her father on the *Titanic,* heiress Peggy Guggenheim became one of the great collectors of the 20th century. Her palatial canalside home, Palazzo Venier dei Leoni, showcases her stockpile of surrealist, futurist and abstract expressionist art with works by up to 200 artists, including her ex-husband Max Ernst, Jackson Pollock (among her many rumoured lovers), Picasso and Salvador Dalí.

★ Basilica di Santa Maria della Salute — BASILICA
(Map p92; www.seminariovenezia.it; Campo della Salute 1b; admission free, sacristy adult/reduced €3/1.50; ☉ 9am-noon & 3-5.30pm; ⛴ Salute) Guarding the entrance to the Grand Canal, this 17th-century domed church was commissioned by Venice's plague survivors as thanks for salvation. Baldassare Longhena's uplifting design is an engineering feat that defies simple logic; in fact, the church is said to have mystical curative properties. Titian eluded the plague until age 94, leaving 12 key paintings in the basilica's art-slung sacristy

★ Scuola Grande di San Rocco — MUSEUM
(Map p92; ☑ 041 523 48 64; www.scuolagrandesanrocco.it; Campo San Rocco 3052, San Polo; adult/reduced €10/8; ☉ 9.30am-5.30pm, Tesoro to 5.15pm; ⛴ San Tomà) Everyone wanted the commission to paint this building dedicated to the patron saint of the plague-stricken, so Tintoretto cheated: instead of producing sketches like rival Veronese, he gifted a splendid ceiling panel of patron St Roch, knowing it couldn't be refused or matched by other artists. The artist documents Mary's life story in the assembly hall, and both Old and New Testament scenes in the Sala Grande Superiore upstairs.

★ Chiesa di Santa Maria dei Miracoli — CHURCH
(Map p92; Campo dei Miracoli 6074; admission €2.50; ☉ 10am-5pm Mon-Sat; ⛴ Fondamenta Nuove) When Nicolò di Pietro's Madonna icon started miraculously weeping in its outdoor shrine around 1480, crowd control became impossible. With pooled resources and marble scavenged from San Marco slag-heaps, neighbours built this chapel (1481–89) to house the painting. Pietro and Tullio Lombardo's miraculous design dropped grandiose Gothic in favour of human-scale harmonies, introducing Renaissance architecture to Venice.

★ Scuola di San Giorgio degli Schiavoni — CHURCH
(Map p92; ☑ 041 522 88 28; Calle dei Furlani 3259a; adult/reduced €5/3; ☉ 2.45-6pm Mon, 9.15am-1pm & 2.45-6pm Tue-Sat, 9.15am-1pm Sun; ⛴ Pietà) Venice's cosmopolitan nature is evident in Castello, where Turkish merchants, Armenian clerics and Balkan and Slavic labourers were considered essential to Venetian commerce and society. This 15th-century religious confraternity headquarters is dedicated to favourite Slavic saints George, Tryphone and Jerome of Dalmatia, whose lives are captured with precision and glowing, early-Renaissance grace by 15th-century master Vittore Carpaccio.

★ Casa dei Tre Oci — CULTURAL CENTRE
(Map p92; ☑ 041 241 23 32; www.treoci.org; Fondamente de la Croce 43; exhibits €5; ☉ 10am-6pm Wed-Mon; ⛴ Zitelle) FREE Acquired by the Fondazione di Venezia in 2000, this fanciful neo-Gothic house was once the home of early-20th-century artist and photographer Mario de Maria, who conceived its distinctive brick facade with its three arched windows

> ### ⓘ SPEEDY ENTRY TO THE BASILICA DI SAN MARCO
>
> The entrances to the Basilica di San Marco are nearly always crowded. Luckily, the queues move quickly – the wait to enter is rarely over 15 minutes, even when the queue extends past the door to Palazzo Ducale. But to abbreviate your wait, consider the following:
>
> ➡ Booking your visit online at www.venetoinside.com (€2 booking fee) allows you to skip the queues.
>
> ➡ Tour groups tend to arrive on the hour or half-hour, so if you arrive outside these times you'll usually have a shorter wait.

Venice

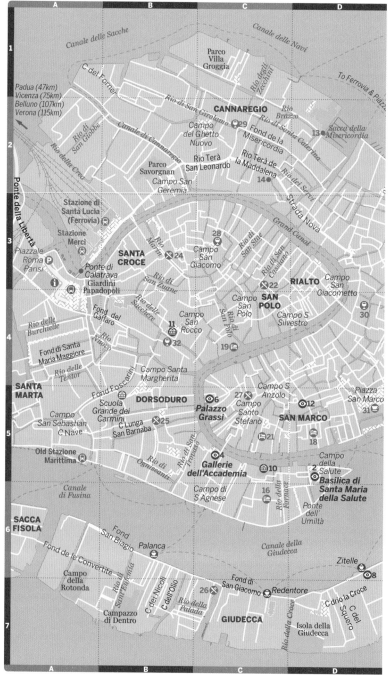

VENICE & PADUA

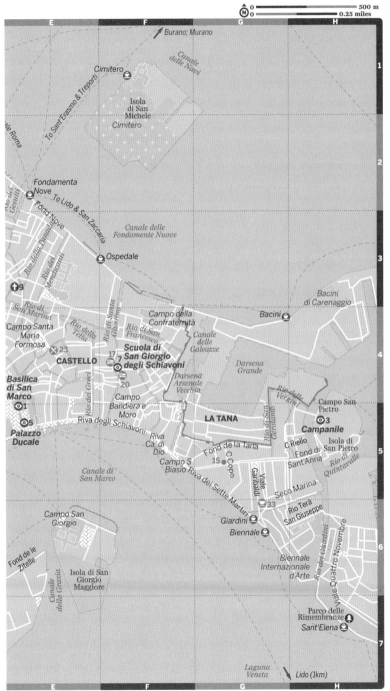

N
0   500 m
0   0.25 miles

To Sant'Erasmo & Treporti

Burano; Murano

Canale
delle Navi

Cimitero

Isola
di San
Michele
Cimitero

Canale delle
Fondamente Nuove

Fondamenta
Nove
To Lido & San Zaccaria

Fond Nove

Ospedale

Bacini
di Carenaggio

Bacini

Campo della
Confraternità

Rio di San
Francesco

Canale
delle
Galeazze

Campo Santa
Maria
Formosa

Scuola di
San Giorgio
degli Schiavoni

Darsena
Grande

23

CASTELLO

17
7
20

Darsena
Arsenale
Vecchia

Basilica
di San
Marco

Campo
Bandiera e
Moro

LA TANA

Campo San
Pietro

Campanile

1

5

Riva degli Schiavoni

Riva
Ca' di
Dio

C Riello

Isola di
San Pietro

3

Palazzo
Ducale

Fond de la Tana

C Copo

Fond di
Sant'Anna

Rio di
Quintavalle

Campo S.
Biasio

15

Riva dei Sette Martiri

Canale di
San Marco

Viale
Garibaldi

Seco Marina

Rio Terà
San Giuseppe

33

Campo San
Giorgio

Giardini

Biennale

Fond de le
Zitelle

Isola di San
Giorgio
Maggiore

Biennale
Internazionale
d'Arte

Parco delle
Rimembranze

Sant'Elena

Laguna
Veneta

Lido (1km)

9

93

Venice

(its namesake 'eyes') in 1910. Now it hosts his photographic archive and fantastic Italian and international exhibitions of contemporary art and photography. The views of San Marco and the Punta della Dogana alone are worth the visit.

🏃 Activities & Tours

A **gondola ride** (☑041 528 50 75; www.gondola venezia.it) gives glimpses into *palazzi* courtyards and canals otherwise unseen on foot. Official daytime rates are €80 for 40 minutes (six passengers maximum), and it's €100 between 7pm and 8am, not including songs (negotiated separately) or tips. Additional time is charged in 20-minute increments (day/night €40/50). Agree on a price, time and singing in advance to avoid surcharges. Gondolas cluster at *stazi* (stops) along the Grand Canal, and at the train station, the Rialto and near monuments, but you can also book a pick-up by calling the main number.

Cheaper shared gondola rides are available through **Tu.Ri.Ve** (www.turive.it), either by booking online or through the tourist office.

Row Venice   ROWING
(Map p92; ☑347 7250637; rowvenice.org; 90min lessons 1-2 people €80, 4 people €120) The next best thing to walking on water: rowing a traditional *batellina coda di gambero* (shrimp-tailed boat) standing up like gondoliers do. Tours must be booked and commence at the

wooden gate of the Sacca Misericordia boat marina at the end of Fondamenta Gasparo Contarini in Cannaregio.

Venice Photo Walk   WALKING TOUR
(☑041 963 73 74; www.msecchi.com; 2/3/6 hr walking tour up to 4 people €210/300/600) Throughout San Marco you'll be tripping over iPhone-touting tourists waving selfie sticks. Everyone, it seems, wants to capture the perfect Venetian scene. Getty photojournalist, Marco Secchi, will show you how.

VeniceArtFactory   CULTURAL TOUR
(Map p92; ☑349 779 93 85, 328 658 38 71; www.veniceartfactory.org; Via Garibaldi 1794; 2-person tour €180, additional adult/student €40/20; 🚇Arsenale) VeniceArtFactory's Studio Tours allow you to sit down to breakfast or share an aperitif with painters, sculptors and engravers in their studios and homes and ask them what it's like to be an artist in the most artful city in the world.

🎉 Festivals & Events

La Biennale di Venezia   CULTURAL
(www.labiennale.org) In odd years the Art Biennale runs from June to October, while in even years the Architecture Biennale runs from September to November. The main venues are Giardini Pubblici pavilions and the Arsenale. Every summer, the Biennale

hosts avant-garde dance, theatre, cinema and music programs throughout the city.

Venice International Film Festival — FILM

(Mostra del Cinema di Venezia; www.labiennale. org/en/cinema) The only thing hotter than a Lido beach in August is the Film Festival's star-studded red carpet, usually rolled out from the last weekend in August through the first week of September.

Regata Storica — CULTURAL

(www.regatastoricavenezia.it) Sixteenth-century costumes, eight-oared gondolas and ceremonial barques feature in this historical procession (usually held in September), which re-enacts the arrival of the Queen of Cyprus and precedes gondola races.

🛏 Sleeping

B&B Corte Vecchia — B&B €

(Map p92; ☑ 041 822 12 33; www.cortevecchia.net; Rio Terà San Vio 462; s €60-100, d €100-130; ✳ 🤶; 🚤 Accademia) Corte Vecchia is a stylish steal, run by young architects Antonella and Mauro and a stone's throw from Peggy Guggenheim and Accademia. Choose from a snug single with en suite, or two good-sized doubles: one with en suite, the other with an external private bathroom. All are simple yet understatedly cool, with contemporary and vintage objects, and a tranquil, shared lounge.

B&B San Marco — B&B €

(Map p92; ☑ 041 522 75 89; www.realvenice.it/ smarco; Fondamente San Giorgio 3385l; d €70-135; ✳ 🤶; 🚤 Pietà, Arsenale) One of the few genuine B&Bs in Venice. Alice and Marco welcome you warmly to their home overlooking Carpaccio's frescoed Scuola di San Giorgio Schiavoni. The 3rd-floor apartment (there is no elevator), with its parquet floors and large, bright windows, is furnished with family antiques and offers photogenic views over the terracotta rooftops and canals. Marco and Alice live upstairs, so they're always on hand with great recommendations.

Hotel Flora — HOTEL €€

(Map p92; ☑ 041 520 58 44; www.hotelflora.it; Calle Bergamaschi 2283a; d €105-365; ✳ 🤶 🤶; 🚤 Santa Maria del Giglio) Down a lane from glitzy Calle Larga XXII Marzo, this ivy-covered retreat quietly outclasses brash designer neighbours with its delightful tearoom, breakfasts around the garden fountain and gym offering shiatsu massage. Guest rooms

Venice's Rialto Bridge at sunrise

feature antique mirrors, hand-carved beds, and tiled en suite baths with apothecary-style amenities. Strollers and kids' teatime complimentary; babysitting available.

Hotel Sant'Antonin — BOUTIQUE HOTEL €€

(Map p92; ☑ 041 523 16 21; www.hotelsant antonin.com; Fondamenta dei Furlani 3299; d €100-280; ✳ 🤶 🤶; 🚤 San Zaccaria) Enjoy the patrician pleasures of a wealthy Greek merchant at this 16th-century *palazzo* perched on a canal near the Greek church. Grand proportions make for light, spacious rooms with cool terrazzo floors, balconies, frescoed ceilings and impressive Baroque furnishings. Come breakfast and you can trip down the stone staircase and out into one of the largest private gardens in Venice. A perfect option for families.

Novecento — BOUTIQUE HOTEL €€€

(Map p92; ☑ 041 241 37 65; www.novecento.biz; Calle del Dose 2683/84; d €160-340; ✳ 🤶; 🚤 Santa Maria del Giglio) Sporting a boho-chic look, the Novecento is a real charmer. Its nine individually designed rooms ooze style with Turkish kilim pillows, Fortuny draperies and 19th-century carved bedsteads. Outside, its garden is a lovely spot to linger over breakfast. Want more? You can go for a massage at sister property Hotel Flora, take a hotel-organised course in landscape drawing, or mingle with creative fellow travellers around the honesty bar.

Hotel Palazzo Barbarigo   DESIGN HOTEL €€€
(Map p92; 041 740 172; www.palazzobarbarigo .com; Grand Canal 2765, San Polo; d €240-440; ❋ 🛜; San Tomà) Brooding, chic and seductive, Barbarigo delivers 18 plush guest rooms combining modern elegance and masquerade intrigue – think dark, contemporary furniture, sumptuous velvets, feathered lamps and the occasional fainting couch. Whether you opt for junior suites overlooking the Grand Canal (get triple-windowed Room 10) or standard rooms overlooking Rio di San Polo, you can indulge in sleek bathrooms, positively royal breakfasts and smart, attentive service.

✖ Eating

Osteria Ruga di Jaffa   OSTERIA €
(Map p92; Ruga Giuffa 4864; meals €20-25; 8am-11pm) Hiding in plain sight on the busy Ruga Giuffa is this excellent *osteria* (casual tavern). You should be able to spot it by the *gondolieri* packing out the tables at lunch time. They may not appreciate the vase of blooming hydrangeas on the bar or the artsy Murano wall lamps, but they thoroughly approve of the select menu of housemade pastas and succulent oven-roast pork soaked in its own savoury juices.

Ristorante La Bitta   RISTORANTE €€
(Map p92; 041 523 05 31; Calle Lunga San Barnaba 2753a; meals €35-40; 6.45-10.45pm Mon-Sat; Ca' Rezzonico) Recalling a cosy, woody bistro, La Bitta keeps punters purring with hearty rustic fare made using the freshest ingredients – the fact that the kitchen has no freezer ensures this. Scan the daily menu for mouthwatering, seasonal options like tagliatelle with artichoke thistle and gorgonzola or juicy pork *salsiccette* (small sausages) served with *verze* (local cabbage) and

warming polenta. Reservations essential. Cash only.

Antiche Carampane   VENETIAN €€
(Map p92; 041 524 01 65; www.antichecaram pane.com; Rio Terà delle Carampane 1911, San Polo; meals €30-45; 12.45-2.30pm & 7.30-10.30pm Tue-Sat; San Stae) Hidden in the once-shady lanes behind Ponte delle Tette, this culinary indulgence is a trick to find. Once you do, say goodbye to soggy lasagne and hello to a market-driven menu of silky *crudi* (raw fish or seafood), surprisingly light *fritto misto* (fried seafood) and prawn salad with seasonal vegetables. Never short of a smart, convivial crowd, it's a good idea to book ahead.

Osteria Trefanti   VENETIAN €€
(Map p92; 041 520 17 89; www.osteriatrefanti.it; Fondamenta Garzotti 888, Santa Croce; meals €40; noon-2.30pm & 7-10.30pm Tue-Sat, noon-2.45pm Sun; 🛜; Riva de Biasio) 🍴 La Serenissima's spice trade lives on at simple, elegant Trefanti, where a vibrant dish of marinated prawns, hazelnuts, berries and caramel might get an intriguing kick from garam masala. Furnished with old pews and recycled copper lamps, it's the domain of the young and competent Sam Metcalfe and Umberto Slongo, whose passion for quality extends to a small, beautifully curated selection of local and organic wines.

Trattoria e Bacaro Da Fiore   VENETIAN, CICHETI €€€
(Map p92; 041 523 53 10; www.dafiore.it; Calle delle Botteghe 3461; meals €45-80, cicheti €10-15; 12.30-2.30pm & 7.30-10.30pm Tue-Sat; San Samuele) Possibly the best bang for your buck in San Marco, this elegant trattoria with its rustic-chic decor serves superlative Venetian dishes composed of carefully selected

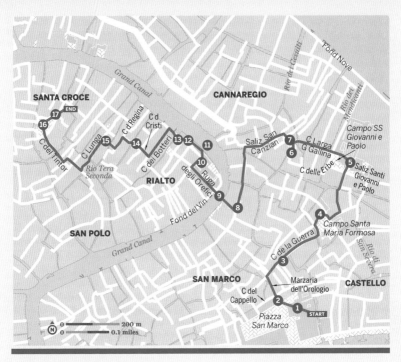

City Walk
Venice Labyrinth

START PIAZZA SAN MARCO
END CAMPO SAN GIACOMO DELL'ORIO
LENGTH 6KM; TWO HOURS

This adventure begins with the obligatory
salute to **①** **Basilica di San Marco** (p43).
Duck under the **②** **Torre dell'Orologio** and
follow the *calle* veering right into **③** **Campo
della Guerra**, where you'll hear Venetian
gossip whispered over *spritz*. Pass over the
bridge along Calle Casselleria into sunny
④ **Campo Santa Maria Formosa**. Straight
ahead is Calle Santa Maria della Formosa; follow it to the left across two bridges to Salizada Santi Giovanni e Paolo, which leads left to
the massive Gothic cathedral, **⑤** **Zanipolo**.

Calle Larga Gallina leads over a bridge;
after this turn left for a glimpse of heaven
at Venice's small wonder, the marble-clad
⑥ **Chiesa di Santa Maria dei Miracoli**
(p91). Backtrack over the bridge to browse
through **⑦** **Campo Santa Maria Nova** to
Salizada San Canzian, which you'll follow
to skinny **⑧** **Chiesa di San Bartolomeo**,

lined with souvenir stalls. To the right is
⑨ **Ponte di Rialto**; stay on the right as you
cross and duck towards happy-hour central,
⑩ **Campo Cesare Battisti**. Continue along
the **⑪** **Grand Canal** to Venice's tastiest
campi: produce-piled **⑫** **Campo Rialto
Mercato** and the covered seafood market,
⑬ **Pescaria**.

Turning left along Calle dei Botteri and
then onto boutique-lined Calle di Cristi, you'll
come to **⑭** **Campo San Cassian**, the site
of the world's first public opera house. Cross
the bridge to Calle della Regina, then head
right to cross another bridge to sociable
⑮ **Chiesa di Santa Maria Mater Dominii**,
with its cafes and ancient neighbourhood
well. Turn left down Calle Lunga and over a
bridge until it dead-ends, then jog left to Rio
Tera Seconda and right again onto Calle del
Tentor. Straight ahead, you'll see the medieval church, **⑯** **San Giacomo dell'Orio**, and
your pick of Italy's best natural-process wines
at **⑰** **Al Prosecco** (p98). *Cin-cin!*

seasonal ingredients from small Veneto producers. Maurizio Martin is justly famous for his seafood dishes such as seabass with balsamic vinegar, although during the Feast of the Redeemer you shouldn't pass up the *castradino* (a sort of Irish stew). Next door serves excellent *cicheti* (bar snacks) at more democratic prices.

Trattoria Altanella
VENETIAN €€€

(Map p92; ☑ 041 522 77 80; Calle delle Erbe 268; meals €35-45; ☺ noon-2.30pm & 7-10.30pm Tue-Sat; ☻ Palanca) In 1920, fisherman Nane Stradella and his wife, Irma, opened a trattoria overlooking the Rio di Ponte Longo. Their fine Venetian cooking was so successful he soon gave up fishing and the restaurant now sustains a fourth generation of family cooks. Inside, the vintage interior is hung with artworks, reflecting the restaurant's popularity with artists, poets and writers, while outside a flower-fringed balcony hangs over the canal. Eat Irma's potato gnocchi with cuttlefish or Nane's enduringly good John Dory fillet.

🍷 Drinking

Bacarando
BAR

(Map p92; ☑ 041 523 82 80; Corte dell'Orso 5495; ☺ 9.30am-midnight; ☻) If you've managed to find this warm, wood-pannelled bar in the warren of streets off San Bartolomeo, toast yourself with a radical rum cocktail (this place has over 150 different labels) and order a huge burger or a plate of heaped *cicheti*. Thanks to its clubby vibe and a lively programme of cultural events and live music, it's popular with a hip young crowd.

Estro
WINE BAR

(Map p92; www.estrovenezia.com; Dorsoduro 3778; ☺ 11am-midnight Wed-Mon, kitchen closes 10pm) New-entry Estro is anything you want it to be: wine and charcuterie bar, *aperitivo* pitstop, or degustation restaurant. The 500 *vini* (wines) – many of them natural-process wines – are chosen by young-gun sibling owners Alberto and Dario, whose passion for quality extends to the grub, from *cicheti* topped with house-made *porchetta* (roast pork), to a succulent burger made with Asiago cheese and house-made ketchup and mayonnaise.

Al Prosecco
WINE BAR

(Map p92; ☑ 041 524 02 22; www.alprosecco.com; Campo San Giacomo dell'Orio, Santa Croce 1503; ☺ 10am-8pm; ☻ San Stae) 🍷 The urge to toast sunsets in Venice's loveliest *campo*

is only natural – and so is the wine at Al Prosecco. This forward-thinking bar specialises in *vini naturi* (natural-process wines) – organic, biodynamic, wild yeast fermented – from enlightened Italian winemakers like Cinque Campi and Azienda Agricola Barichel. So order a glass of unfiltered 'cloudy' prosecco and toast to the good things in life

Al Timon
WINE BAR

(Map p92; ☑ 041 524 60 66; Fondamenta degli Ormesini 2754; ☺ 11am-1am Thu-Tue & 6pm-1am Wed; ☻ San Marcuola) Find a spot on the boat moored on the canal and watch the motley parade of drinkers and dreamers arrive for seafood *crostini* (open-face sandwiches) and quality organic and DOC wines by the *ombra* (half-glass of winc) or carafe. Folk singers play sets canalside when the weather obliges; when it's cold, regulars scoot over to make room for newcomers at indoor tables.

Caffè Florian
CAFE

(Map p92; ☑ 041 520 56 41; www.caffeflorian.com; Piazza San Marco 56/59; drinks €10-25; ☺ 9am-midnight; ☻ San Marco) One of Venice's most famous cafes, Florian maintains rituals (if not prices) established c 1720: white-jacketed waiters serve cappuccino on silver trays, lovers canoodle in plush banquettes and the orchestra strikes up a tango as the sunset illuminates San Marco's mosaics.

La Serra dei Giardini
CAFE

(Map p92; ☑ 041 296 03 60; www.serradeigiardini.org; Viale Giuseppe Garibaldi 1254; snacks €4-15; ☺ 10am-9.30pm summer, 11am-8pm Mon-Thu & 10am-9pm Fri & Sat winter; 🛜 📵; ☻ Giardini) Order a herbal tisane or the signature pear Bellini and sit back amid the hothouse flowers in Napoleon's fabulous greenhouse. Cathedral-like windows look out onto the tranquil greenery of the public gardens, while upstairs workshops in painting and gardening are hosted on the suspended mezzanine. Light snacks and cakes are also available alongside unique micro-brews and Lurisia sodas flavoured with Slow Food Presidia products.

ℹ️ Information

EMERGENCY

For an ambulance, call ☑ 118. Call ☑ 112 or ☑ 113 for the police.

Police Headquarters (☑ 041 271 55 11; Santa Croce 500) San Marco's head police station is off the beaten track in the ex-convent of Santa Chiara, just beyond Piazzale Roma.

The Basilica di Santa Maria della Salute (p91) looms large over Venice's Grand Canal

MEDICAL SERVICES

Information on rotating late-night pharmacies is posted in pharmacy windows and listed in the free magazine *Un Ospite di Venezia,* available at the tourist office.

Guardia Medica (☑ 041 238 56 48) This service of night-time call-out doctors in Venice operates from 8pm to 8am on weekdays and from 10am the day before a holiday (including Sunday) until 8am the day after.

Ospedale Civile (☑ 041 529 41 11; Campo SS Giovanni e Paolo 6777; ☒ Ospedale) Venice's main hospital; for emergency care and dental treatment.

TOURIST INFORMATION

Airport Tourist Office (☑ 041 529 87 11; www. turismovenezia.it; Arrivals Hall, Marco Polo Airport; ☺ 8.30am-7.30pm)

❶ Getting There & Away

CAR & MOTORCYCLE

The congested Trieste–Turin A4 passes through Mestre. From Mestre, take the Venice exit. From the south, take the A13 from Bologna, which connects with the A4 at Padua.

Once over the Ponte della Libertà bridge from Mestre, cars must be left at the car park at Piazzale Roma or Tronchetto; expect to pay €21 or more for every 24 hours. Parking stations in Mestre are cheaper. Car ferry 17 transports vehicles from Tronchetto to the Lido.

Avis, Europcar and Hertz all have car rental offices on Piazzale Roma and at Marco Polo airport. Several companies operate in or near Mestre train station, too.

Interparking (Tronchetto Car Park; ☑ 041 520 75 55; www.veniceparking.it; Isola del Tronchetto; per 2/3-5/5-24hr €3/5/21; ☺ 24hr) Has 3957 spaces; the largest lot with the cheapest 24-hour rate. *Vaporetti* connect directly with Piazza San Marco, while the People Mover provides connections to Piazzale Roma and the cruise terminal.

❶ Getting Around

VAPORETTO

The city's main mode of public transport is *vaporetto* – Venice's distinctive water bus. Tickets can be purchased from the HelloVenezia ticket booths at most landing stations. You can also buy tickets when boarding; you may be charged double with luggage, though this is not always enforced.

Instead of spending €7 for a one-way ticket, consider a Travel Card, which is a timed pass for unlimited travel (beginning at first validation). Passes for 24/48/72 hours cost €20/30/40. A week pass costs €60.

WATER TAXIS

The standard **water taxi** (Consorzio Motoscafi Venezia; 24hr ☑ 041 522 23 03, Marco Polo airport desk ☑ 041 541 50 84; www.motos-cafivenezia.it) between Marco Polo airport and Venice costs €110 for a private taxi and €25 per person for a shared taxi with up to 10 passengers. Elsewhere in Venice, official taxi rates start at €15 plus €2 per minute and €6 extra if they're called to your hotel. Night trips, extra luggage and large groups cost more. Prices are metered or negotiated in advance.

PADUA

POP 209,700

Though under an hour from Venice, Padua seems a world away with its medieval marketplaces, Fascist-era facades and hip student population. As a medieval city-state and home to Italy's second-oldest university, Padua challenged both Venice and Verona for regional hegemony. An extraordinary series of fresco cycles recalls this golden age – including in Giotto's remarkable Cappella degli Scrovegni, Menabuoi's heavenly gathering in the Baptistry and Titian's St Anthony in the Scoletta del Santo. For the next few centuries Padua and Verona challenged each other for dominance over the Veneto plains. But Venice finally settled the matter by occupying Padua permanently in 1405.

As a strategic military-industrial centre, Padua became a parade ground for Mussolini speeches, an Allied bombing target and a secret Italian Resistance hub.

◉ Sights

★ **Cappella degli Scrovegni**　　　　CHURCH
See p42.

Padua

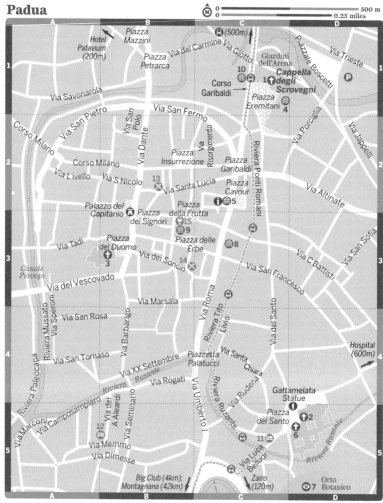

Musei Civici agli Eremitani
MUSEUM

(Map p100; ☑049 820 45 51; Piazza Eremitani 8; adult/reduced €10/8; ⊙9am-7pm Tue-Sun) The ground floor of this monastery houses artefacts dating from Padua's Roman and pre-Roman past. Upstairs, a rambling but interesting collection boasts a few notable 14th- to 18th-century works by Bellini, Giorgione, Tintoretto and Veronese. Among the show-stoppers is a crucifix by Giotto, showing a heartbroken Mary wringing her hands as Jesus' blood drips into the empty eye sockets of a human skull.

Mary also appears in a series of dazzling paintings by 14th-century artist Guariento di Arpo, executed for the private chapel of Padua's powerful Carraresi (da Carrara) family.

Palazzo Zuckermann
GALLERY

(Map p100; ☑049 820 56 64; Corso di Garibaldi 33; adult/reduced €10/8; ⊙10am-7pm Tue-Sun) The ground and 1st floors of the early-20th-century Palazzo Zuckermann are home to the **Museo d'Arti Applicate e Decorative**, whose eclectic assortment of decorative and applied arts spans several centuries of flatware, furniture, fashion and jewellery. On the 2nd floor is the **Museo Bottacin**, a treasury of finely worked historic coins and medals, kept company by a modest collection of 19th-century paintings and sculpture.

Padua

Palazzo del Bò
HISTORIC BUILDING

(Map p100; ☑049 827 30 47; www.unipd.it/en/ guidedtours; Via VIII Febbraio; adult/reduced €5/2; ⊙see website for tour times) This Renaissance *palazzo* is the seat of Padua's history-making university. Founded by renegade scholars from Bologna seeking greater intellectual freedom, the university has employed some of Italy's greatest and most controversial thinkers, including Copernicus, Galileo, Casanova and the world's first female doctor of philosophy, Eleonora Lucrezia Cornaro Piscopia (her statue graces the stairs). The 45-minute guided tours include the world's first **anatomy theatre**.

Palazzo della Ragione
HISTORIC BUILDING

(Map p100; ☑049 820 50 06; Piazza delle Erbe; adult/ reduced €4/2; ⊙9am-7pm Tue-Sun, to 6pm Nov-Jan) Ancient Padua can be glimpsed in elegant twin squares separated by the Gothic Palazzo della Ragione, the city's tribunal dating from 1218. Inside Il Salone (the Great Hall), frescoes by Giotto acolytes Giusto de' Menabuoi and Nicolò Miretto depict the astrological theories of Paduan professor Pietro d'Abano, with images representing the months, seasons, saints, animals and noteworthy Paduans (not necessarily in that order).

The enormous 15th-century wooden horse at the western end of the hall was modelled on Donatello's majestic bronze *Gattamelata*, which still stands in Piazza del Santo. At the other end of the hall is a contemporary version of Foucault's *Pendulum*.

Duomo
CATHEDRAL

(Map p100; ☑049 65 69 14; Piazza del Duomo; baptistry €3; ⊙7.30am-noon & 4-7.30pm Mon-Sat, 8am-1pm & 4-8.45pm Sun & holidays, baptistry 10am-6pm) Built from a much-altered design of Michelangelo's, the whitewashed symmetry of Padua's cathedral is a far cry from its rival in Piazza San Marco. Pop in quickly for Giuliano Vangi's contemporary chancel crucifix and sculptures before taking in the adjoining 13th-century baptistry, a Romanesque gem frescoed with luminous biblical scenes by Giusto de' Menabuoi. Hundreds of male and female saints congregate in the cupola, posed as though for a school photo, exchanging glances and stealing looks at the Madonna.

Basilica di Sant'Antonio
CHURCH

(Map p100; Il Santo; ☑049 822 56 52; www.basili-cadelsanto.org; Piazza del Santo; ⊙6.20am-7.45pm Apr-Oct, to 6.45pm Nov-Mar) **FREE** Il Santo is the soul of Padua, a key pilgrimage site and the burial place of patron saint St Anthony of

Market in Piazza delle Erbe at dusk

Padua (1193–1231). Begun in 1232, its polyglot style incorporates rising eastern domes atop a Gothic brick structure crammed with Renaissance treasures. Behind the high altar nine radiating chapels punctuate a broad ambulatory homing in on the Cappella del Tesoro (Treasury Chapel), where the relics of St Anthony reside.

Oratorio di San Giorgio & Scoletta del Santo
CHURCH

(Map p100; ☎ 049 822 56 52; Piazza del Santo; adult/reduced €5/4; ⊗ 9am-12.30pm & 2.30-7pm Apr-Sep, to 5pm Oct-Mar) Anywhere else the fresco cycle of the Oratorio di San Giorgio and the paintings in the Scoletta del Santo would be considered highlights, but in Padua they must contend with Giotto's Scrovegni brilliance. This means you'll have Altichiero da Zevio and Jacopo Avanzi's jewel-like, 14th-century frescoes of St George, St Lucy and St Catherine all to yourself, while upstairs in the *scoletta* (confraternity house), Titian paintings are seldom viewed in such tranquillity.

Orto Botanico
GARDENS

(Map p100; ☎ 049 201 02 22; www.ortobotanicopd.it; Via dell'Orto Botanico 15; adult/reduced €10/8; ⊗ 9am-7pm daily Apr & May, 9am-7pm Tue-Sun Jun-Sep, to 6pm Tue-Sun Oct, to 5pm Tue-Sun Nov-Mar; ☎ ♿) Planted in 1545 by Padua University's medical faculty to study the medicinal properties of rare plants, Padua's World Heritage–listed Orto Botanico served as a clandestine Resistance meeting head-

quarters in WWII. The oldest tree is nicknamed 'Goethe's palm'; planted in 1585, it was mentioned by the great German writer in his *Voyage in Italy*. A much more recent addition is the high-tech Garden of Biodiversity, five interconnected greenhouses that recreate different climate zones and explore botanical and environmental themes via multimedia displays.

🛏 Sleeping

The tourist office publishes accommodation brochures and lists dozens of B&Bs, apartments and hotels online.

Ostello Città di Padova
HOSTEL €

(Map p100; ☎ 049 875 22 19; www.ostellopadova.it; Via dei Aleardi 30; dm €19-23, d €46, without bathroom €40; ⊗ reception 7.15-9.30am & 3.30-11.30pm; ☎) A central hostel with decent four- and six-bed dorm rooms on a quiet side street. Sheets and wi-fi are free. Breakfast is served between 7.30am and 8.30am, though there is no open kitchen. There's an 11.30pm curfew, except when there are special events, and guests must check out by 9.30am. Take bus 12 or 18, or the tram from the train station.

Belludi37
BOUTIQUE HOTEL €€

(Map p100; ☎ 049 66 56 33; www.belludi37.it; Via Luca Belludi 37; s €80, d €140-180; ❄ ☎) Graced with Flos bedside lamps and replica Danish chairs, the neutrally toned rooms at Belludi37 feature high ceilings, queen-sized beds and free minibar. Six new rooms also deliver svelte bathrooms. Extra perks include a central location and staff always on hand with suggestions for biking routes and walking tours.

✖ Eating

Zairo ITALIAN €

(☑049 66 38 03; http://zairo.net; Prato della Valle 51; pizzas €4-9.40, meals €25; ⊙noon-2pm & 7pm-midnight Tue-Sun) The fresco above the kitchen door at this sweeping, chintzy restaurant-pizzeria dates back to 1673. But you're here for Zairo's cult hit *gnocchi verdi con gorgonzola* (spinach and potato gnocchi drizzled in a decadent gorgonzola sauce), or one of its decent, spot-hitting pizzas.

Osteria dei Fabbri OSTERIA €€

(Map p100; ☑049 65 03 36; Via dei Fabbri 13; meals €30; ⊙noon-2.30pm & 7-10.30pm Mon-Sat, noon-3pm Sun) Communal tables, wine-filled tumblers and a single-sheet menu packed with hearty dishes keep things real at dei Fabbri. Slurp on superlative *zuppe* (soups) like sweet red-onion soup, or tuck into comforting meat dishes such as oven-roasted pork shank with Marsala, sultanas and polenta.

★ Belle Parti ITALIAN €€€

(Map p100; ☑049 875 18 22; www.ristorante-belleparti.it; Via Belle Parti 11; meals €50; ⊙12.30-2.30pm & 7.30-10.30pm Mon-Sat) Prime seasonal produce, impeccable service and near-faultless service meld into one unforgettable whole at this stellar fine-dining restaurant, resplendent with 18th-century antiques and 19th-century oil paintings. Seafood is the forte, with standout dishes including an arresting *gran piatto di crudità di mare* (raw seafood platter). Dress to impress and book ahead.

⚇ Drinking & Entertainment

Sundown isn't official until you've enjoyed a *spritz* in Piazza delle Erbe or Piazza dei Signori. Also note that Padua is the region's unofficial capital of gay and lesbian life.

Caffè Pedrocchi CAFE

(Map p100; ☑049 878 12 31; www.caffepedrocchi.it; Via VIII Febbraio 15; ⊙8.45am-midnight Apr-Oct, to 11pm Nov-Mar) Divided into three rooms – red, white and green – the neoclassical Pedrocchi has long been a seat of intrigue and revolution, as well as a favourite of Stendhal. Soak up its history over coffee or head in for a sprightly *spritz* and decent *aperitivo* snacks.

Decorated in styles ranging from ancient Egyptian to Imperial, the building's 1st floor is home to the Museo del Risorgimento e dell'Età Contemporanea (☑049 878 12 31; Galleria Pedrocchi 11; adult/child €4/2.50; ⊙9.30am-12.30pm & 3.30-6pm Tue-Sun), which recounts local and national history from the fall of Venice in 1797 until the republican constitution of 1848.

Enoteca Il Tira Bouchon WINE BAR

(Map p100; ☑049 875 21 38; www.enotecapadova.it; Sotto il Salone 23/24; ⊙10am-2.30pm & 5-9pm Mon-Sat) With a French hand behind the bar you can be sure of an excellent *prosecco*, Franciacorta or sauvignon at this traditional wine bar beneath Palazzo Ragione's arcades. Locals crowd in for *spunci* (bread-based snacks), *panini* and a rotating selection of 12 wines by the glass. You'll find around 300 wines on the shelves, including emerging winemakers.

ⓘ Information

Hospital (☑049 821 11 11; Via Giustiniani 1) Main public hospital.

Police Station (☑049 83 31 11; Piazzetta Palatucci 5)

Tourist Office (☑049 201 00 80; www.turismopadova.it; Vicolo Pedrocchi; ⊙9am-7pm Mon-Sat) Ask about the PadovaCard here. There is a second **tourist office** (☑049 201 00 80; Piazza di Stazione; ⊙9am-7pm Mon-Sat, 10am-4pm Sun) at the train station.

ⓘ Getting Around

TRAM

It is easy to get to all the sights by foot from the train and bus stations, but the city's single-branch tram running from the train station passes within 100m of all the main sights. Tickets (€1.30) are available at tobacconists and newsstands.

The two semi-autonomous provinces of Trentino and Alto Adige offer up a number of stunning wilderness areas, where adventure and comfort can be found in equal measure. Wooden farmhouses dot vine- and orchard-covered valleys and the region's cities are easy to navigate, cultured and fun.

Trento

POP 117,300 / ELEV 194M

Modern Trento is a quietly confident, liberal and easy-to-like place. Bicycles glide along spotless streets fanning out from the atmospheric, intimate Piazza del Duomo, students clink *spritzes* by Renaissance fountains and a dozen historical eras intermingle seamlessly amid stone castles, shady porticoes and the city's signature medieval frescoes. While there's no doubt you're in Italy, Trento does have its share of Austrian influence: apple strudel is ubiquitous and beer halls not uncommon. Set in a wide glacial valley guarded by the crenulated peaks of the Brenta Dolomites, amid a patchwork of vineyards and apple orchards, Trento is a perfect jumping-off point for hiking, skiing or wine tasting. And road cycling is huge: 400km of paved cycling paths fan out from here.

◉ Sights

Helpful plaques indicate which historical era various buildings belong to – often several at once in this many-layered city.

★ MUSE   MUSEUM

(Museo della Scienze; ☑ 0461 27 03 11; www.muse.
it; Corso del Lavoro e della Scienza 3; adult/reduced
€10/8, guided tours (in English by appointment)
€3; ☉ 10am-6pm Tue-Fri, to 9pm Wed, to 7pm Sat
& Sun; ⓘ) ⟋ A stunning new architectural work, care of Renzo Piano, houses this 21st-century science museum and cleverly echoes the local landscape. Curatorially, the museum typifies the city's brainy inquisitiveness, with highly interactive exhibitions that explore the Alpine environment, biodiversity and sustainability, society and technology. Highlights are a truly amazing collection of taxidermy, much of it suspended in a multistorey atrium, along with a fabulous experiential kids area and open working **laboratories** (☉ visits 11.30am-noon, 3-3.30pm Wed-Fri).

Castello del Buonconsiglio   MUSEUM
See p50.

Duomo   CATHEDRAL
(Map p106; Cattedrale di San Vigilio; ☉ 6.30am-6pm) Once host to the Council of Trent, this dimly lit Romanesque cathedral displays fragments of medieval frescoes inside its transepts. Two colonnaded stairways flank the nave, leading, it seems, to heaven. Built over a 6th-century temple devoted to San Vigilio, patron saint of Trento, the foundations form part of a palaeo-Christian **archaeological area** (adult/reduced incl with nearby Museo Diocesano €5/3; ☉ 10am-noon & 2.30-5.30pm Mon-Sat).

🏃 Activities

For suggested walking itineraries, and information on *vie ferrate* (trails with permanent cables and ladders) and *rifugi* (mountain huts), visit the local Società degli Alpinisti Tridentini (SAT; ☑0461 98 28 04; www.sat.tn.it; Palazzo Saracini Cresseri, Via Manci 57; ⊙9am-noon & 3-7pm Mon-Fri, afternoons only in winter), staffed by friendly mountaineers.

☞ Tours

The tourist office runs two-hour multilingual walking tours (€6) every Saturday, visiting Castello del Buonconsiglio at 10am or around the town centre at 3pm. The afternoon slot finishes with a Trento DOC sparkling tasting at the Palazzo Roccabruno.

🛏 Sleeping

Central hotels book out in early June, when the Festival Economia (2012.festivaleconomia.eu) comes to town, and during other conferences. Agritur Trentino (☑0461 23 53 23; www.agriturismotrentino.com; Via Aconcio 13; ⊙9am-noon Mon-Fri) can put you in touch with rural B&Bs and *agriturismi* (farm stay accommodation), often only a short drive from the centre.

Al Cavour 34   B&B €
(Map p106; www.alcavour34.it; Via Cavour 34; s/d €70/100; ✽🖂) This little B&B is run by a young couple, both five-star hospitality veterans, who infuse all with a wonderful mix of genuine warmth and absolute professionalism. Rooms are large and decorated in a contemporary style; breakfast is taken around a large table with daily surprises from the local baker or home-baked treats like cookies or apple crumble.

Ostello Giovane Europa   HOSTEL €
(Map p106; ☑0461 26 34 84; www.gayaproject.org; Via Torre Vanga 9; dm/s/d €17/28/45, single night stays €2 extra; ⊙reception closed 10am-2pm; 🖂) Squeaky-clean rooms are comfortable and upper floors have mountain views; the mansard-roofed family room on the top floor is particularly spacious. While it's conveniently located, it can get noisy.

Albergo Accademia   HOTEL €€
(Map p106; ☑0461 23 36 00; www.accademiahotel.it; Vicolo Colico 4/6; s/d €89/120; 🅿✽@) Elegant small hotel in a historic medieval house with rooms that are modern and airy (if a little on the staid side). Suites are luxuriously

ℹ TRENTOROVERETO CARD

Available from the tourist office and some museums, this card (adult plus one child €20, 48 hours) gets you free entry to all city and regional museums and the Botanical Alpine Gardens, as well as wine tastings and walking tours, bike hire and free public transport – including the Trento–Sardagna cable car and regional trains and buses. Register online and the card lasts a further three months, free transport aside.

spacious, including one with a large private terrace and sauna.

🍴 Eating & Drinking

Trento's table is a hearty one and draws many of its ingredients – beef, game, cheese, mushrooms – from its fertile hinterland. There's a lot of cross-cultural traffic too: *cotoletta* (schnitzel) and *canederli* (dumplings) are decidedly Tyrolean, polenta and asparagus evoke the Veneto, and Garda's olive oil conjures the Mediterranean. Bakeries brim with apple strudel, but don't overlook the local carrot cake. Wines to look out for include Trento DOC, a sparkling wine made from chardonnay grapes, the white Nosiola and the extremely drinkable red, Teroldego Rotaliano DOC. Trentino's smartly bottled Surgiva mineral water is considered one of Italy's best, for taste and purity.

Moki   MODERN ITALIAN €
(Map p106; ☑347 0431426; www.moki-trento.it; Via Malpaga 20; meals €23; ⊙9am-8pm Mon, 9am-10pm Tue-Sat) A warren of bright white rooms, welcoming staff, new ideas and a stack of great magazines make Moki a perfect choice for breakfast, lunch or an *aperitivo* (if there's a bottle of the pink Revi Trento DOC open, don't say no). Dinners on Friday and Saturday nights begin with 'tapas' style platters and the fresh, tasty mains always include a vegetarian option.

Pedavena   BREWERY €
(Map p106; ☑0461 98 62 55; Piazza di Fiera 13; meals €20-30; ⊙Wed-Mon 9am-midnight, to 1am Fri & Sat) Proudly crowd-pleasing and perennially popular, this sprawling 1920s beer hall (complete with fermenting brew in the corner) serves up the comfort food you'd expect: bratwurst, schnitzel and steaming

Trento

Trento

◎ Sights
1 Castello del Buonconsiglio	D2
2 Duomo	C4

◉ Sleeping
3 Al Cavour 34	B3
4 Albergo Accademia	B3
5 Ostello Giovane Europa	B2

◎ Eating
6 Il Cappello	D2

7 Moki	C3
8 Pedavena	C4
9 Scrigno del Duomo	C3

◎ Drinking & Nightlife
10 Casa del Caffe	C3

◎ Shopping
11 Raccolta Differenziata	C3

plates of polenta with mushroom stew and slabs of melty white *tosella* cheese.

★ **Scrigno del Duomo** GASTRONOMIC €€
(Map p106; ☑ 0461 22 00 30; www.scrignodelduomo.com; Piazza del Duomo 29; meals €35, degustation from €55; ☉ wine bar 11am-2.30pm & 6-11pm, dining room 12.30-2.30pm & 7.30-10pm Tue-Sun, dinner only Sat) Trento's culinary and social epicentre is discreetly housed in a building dating back to the 1200s. For degustation dining take the stairs down to the formal restaurant, with its glassed-in Roman-era cellar. Or stay upstairs underneath the beautiful painted wooden ceiling, where there's simple, stylishly done local specialities.

Il Cappello TRENTINO €€
(Map p106; ☑ 0461 23 58 50; www.osteriailcappello. it; Piazzetta Lunelli 5; meals €35; ☉ noon-2.30pm

& 7-10pm Tue-Sat, noon-3pm Sun) This intimate dining room has an unexpectedly rustic feel, with wooden beams and a terrace set in a quiet courtyard. The menu is Trentino to the core, and simple presentation makes the most of beautiful artisan produce. Wines too are local and rather special.

Casa del Caffe CAFE
(Map p106; Via San Pietro 38; ⊙ 7.30am-12.30pm & 3-7.30pm Mon-Sat) Follow your nose to this coffee bar and chocolate shop for Trento's best espresso. Beans are roasted on the premises and the crowded shelves feature some of the country's best boutique products.

Osteria della Mal'Ombra BAR
(www.osteriadellamalombra.com; Corso III Novembre 43; ⊙ 8.30am-2.30pm & 3.30pm-midnight Mon-Fri, 4pm-1am Sat) Join the university set for good wine and grappa, possibly some spirited political debate, and music on Tuesdays.

🛍 Shopping

Raccolta Differenziata FASHION
(Map p106; ☑ 0461 26 12 92; Via Malpaga 16-18; ⊙ 3pm-7pm Mon, 11am-7pm Tue-Sat) Luigi Andreis has long been Trento's super stylist and it's worth seeking out his shop, tucked away in a quiet courtyard of an ancient *palazzo* from the 1400s, to experience his fascinating eye and treat yourself to one of the beautiful pieces from mostly Italian designers.

ℹ Information

Hospital (☑ 0461 90 31 11; Largo Medaglie d'Oro 9)

Police Station (☑ 0461 89 95 11; Piazza della Mostra 3)

Post Office (Piazza Vittoria; ⊙ 8am-6.30pm Mon-Fri, to 12.30pm Sat)

Tourist Office (☑ 0461 21 60 00; www.apt. trento.it; Via Manci 2; ⊙ 9am-7pm)

Rovereto

POP 37,550

When Leopold Mozart and his soon-to-be-famous musical son visited Rovereto in the winter of 1769, they found it to be 'rich in diligent people engaged in viticulture and the weaving of silk'. The area is no longer known for silk, but still produces some outstanding wines, including the inky, cherry-scented Marzemino (the wine's scene-stealing appearance in *Don Giovanni* suggests it may have been a Mozart family favourite). Those on a musical pilgrimage come for the annual Mozart Festival (www. festivalmozartrovereto.it; ⊙ Jul) in August. It is arguably the shock of the new, though, that is now the town's greatest lure: Rovereto is home to one of Italy's best contemporary and 20th-century art museums.

👁 Sights

★ **Museo di Arte Moderna e Contemporanea Rovereto** ART GALLERY
(MART; ☑ 0464 43 88 87; english.mart.trento.it; Corso Bettini 43; adult/reduced €11/7, incl Casa del Depero €13/9; ⊙ 10am-6pm Tue-Thu, Sat & Sun, to 9pm Fri) The four-floor, 12,000-sq-metre steel, glass and marble behemoth, care of the Ticinese architect Mario Botta, is both imposing and human in scale, with mountain light gently filling a central atrium from a soaring cupola. It's home to some huge 20th-century works, including Warhol's *Four Marilyns* (1962), several Picassos and a clutch of contemporary art stars, including Bill Viola, Kara Walker, Arnuf Rainer and a whopping-great Anslem Keifer.

Casa del Depero MUSEUM
(☑ 0424 60 04 35; Via Portici 38; adult/reduced €7/4, incl MART admission €13/9; ⊙ 10am-6pm Tue-Sun) Those Futurists were never afraid of a spot of self-aggrandisement and local lad Fortunato Depero was no exception. This self-designed museum was first launched shortly before his death in 1960, and was then restored and reopened by MART in recent years. The obsessions of early-20th-century Italy mix nostalgically, somewhat unnervingly, with a historic past – bold tapestries and machine-age-meets-troubadour-era furniture decorate a made-over medieval town house.

Church of San Marco CHURCH
See p50.

🍴 Eating & Drinking

Osteria del Pettirosso WINE BAR
(www.osteriadelpettirosso.com; Corso Bettini 24; ⊙ 10am-11pm Mon-Sat) There's a moody downstairs dining room but most people come here for the blackboard menu of wines by the glass, many from small producers, a plate of cheese (€8) or a couple of *crostone all lardo* (toasts with cured pork fat).

ⓘ Information

Tourist Office (☎ 0464 43 03 63; www.
visitrovereto.it; Piazza Rosmini 16; ⊙9am-1pm
& 2-6pm Mon-Sat, 10am-4pm Sun) The tourist
office has lots of information on Rovereto, town
maps and details of cycling trails.

Bolzano (Bozen)

POP 103,500 / ELEV 265M

The provincial capital of Alto Adige (Südtirol, or South Tyrol) is anything but provincial. Its quality of life – one of the highest in
Italy – is reflected in its openness, youthful
energy and an all-pervading greenness. A
stage-set-pretty backdrop of rotund green
hills sets off rows of pastel-painted town
houses. Bicycles ply riverside paths and
wooden market stalls are laid out with Alpine cheese, speck (cured ham) and dark,
seeded loaves. German may be the first
language of 95% of the region, but Bolzano
is an anomaly. Today its Italian-speaking
majority – a legacy of Mussolini's brutal
Italianisation program of the 1920s and the
more recent siren call of education and em-
ployment opportunities – looks both north
and south for inspiration.

◉ Sights

★ Museo Archeologico dell'Alto
Adige   MUSEUM

(Map p109; ☎ 0471 32 01 00; www.iceman.it; Via Museo 43; adult/reduced €9/7; ⊙10am-6pm Tue-Sun)
The star of the Museo Archeologico dell'Alto Adige is Ötzi, the Iceman, with almost
the entire museum being given over to the
Copper Age mummy. Kept in a temperature-
controlled 'igloo' room, he can be viewed
through a small window (peer closely
enough and you can make out faintly visible tattoos on his legs). Ötzi's clothing – a
wonderful get-up of patchwork leggings,
rush-matting cloak and fur cap – and other
belongings are also displayed.

Messner Mountain Museum   MUSEUM

(MMM Firmian; ☎ 0471 63 31 45; www.messner-
mountain-museum.it; Via Castel Firmiano 53; adult/
reduced €10/8; ⊙10am-6pm Fri-Wed Mar-Nov)
The imposing Castel Firmiano, dating back
to AD 945, is the centrepiece of mountaineer
Reinhold Messner's five museums. Based
around humankind's relationship with the
mountains across all cultures, the architecture itself suggests the experience of shifting
altitudes, and requires visitors to traverse

hundreds of stairs and mesh walkways.
The collection is idiosyncratic, but when it
works, it's heady stuff. Messner's other museums are scattered across the region, including Ortles.

There's a shuttle from Piazza Walther
in summer, or you can catch a taxi or
take the suburban train to Ponte Adige/
Sigmundskron (beware there is then a long
walk up a truck-laden road).

Museion   ART GALLERY

(Map p109; ☎ 0471 22 34 13; www.museion.it; Via
Dante 2; adult/reduced €7/3.50, Thu from 6pm free;
⊙10am-6pm Tue-Sun, to 10pm Thu) The city's
contemporary art space is housed in a huge
multifaceted glass cube, a brave architectural surprise that beautifully vignettes the
old-town rooftops and surrounding mountains from within. There's an impressive
permanent collection of international artwork; temporary shows are a testament to
the local art scene's vibrancy, or often highlight an ongoing dialogue with artists and
institutions from Austria and Germany. The
river-facing cafe has a terrace perfect for a
post-viewing *spritz*.

🏃 Activities

Bolzano's trio of cable cars whisk you up out
of the city, affording spectacular views over
the city and valley floor, then of terraced
vineyards, tiny farms, ancient mountain
chapels and towering peaks beyond. The re-
spective villages are delightful destinations
in themselves or jumping off points for ram-
bles or serious hikes. Walks can also be done
from the city centre – ask at the tourist office
for the map marked with the routes to Santa
Maddalena and San Osvaldo.

Funivia del Renon   CABLE CAR

(Via Renon; one way/return €6/10) The journey over the Renon (Ritten) plateau to
Soprabolzano (Oberbozen) runs along the
world's longest single track, stretching
for 4.56km, passing over eerie red earth
pyramids.

Funivia del Colle   CABLE CAR

(Via Campegno 4; one way/return €4/6) This is
the world's oldest cable car, dreamt up by a
canny inn-keeper in 1908, with a pristine village awaiting at the top.

Funivia San Genesio   CABLE CAR

(Via Sarentino; one way/return €3/5) An ultra-
steep ascent takes you to the beautiful terraced village of San Genesio (Jenesien),

Bolzano

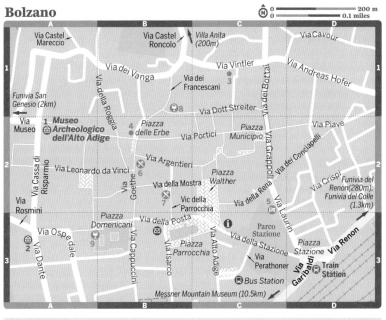

Bolzano

where there are roof-of-the-world views and forest trails to follow.

🛏 Tours

The tourist office organises free city tours in English and seasonal guided walks and gentle treks in Italian and German. For serious hiking information, contact one of the local walking associations.

Club Alpino Italiano   WALKING

(📞 0471 97 81 72; Piazza delle Erbe 46; ⊙ 11am-1pm & 5-7pm Wed, 1-5pm Tue, Thu & Fri)

Alpine Information Office   WALKING

(Map p109; Alpenverein Südtirol; 📞 0471 81 41 55; www.alpenverein.it; Galleria Vintler 16)

🛏 Sleeping

Villa Anita   GUESTHOUSE €

(Via Castel Roncolo 16; d/family €68/75 shared bathroom; 🅿🛜) Although it's just a short walk from the historic centre, the surrounding gardens make this beautiful 1905 villa seem like you're already out in the countryside. Rooms are spacious and light, the shared bathrooms are modern and spotlessly maintained and the owner is gracious and kind. You can pay a little extra for a room with a balcony or for a self-catering apartment.

★**Parkhotel Laurin**   HOTEL €€€

(📞 0471 31 10 00; www.laurin.it; Via Laurin 4; s €95-125, d €130-250; 🅿❄🛜🏊) Set in its own lush gardens in the centre of town, this five-star hotel has large rooms endowed with a weighty, old-fashioned opulence and staff that mesh haute-professionalism with relaxed Alpine charm. There's a distinct individual style and contemporary sensibility throughout though, with an idiosyncratic mix of original artworks, Tyrolean antiques and 1980s Memphis pieces.

The splendid ground floor is home to what's considered one of Bolzano's best restaurants and a dark baronial bar that bustles from early morning to late at night.

✗ Eating

Redolent of rural mountain life one minute, Habsburg splendour the next, Bolzano's restaurants – often in the guise of a traditional wood-panelled dining room called a *stube* – are a profound reminder of just how far north you've come.

Vögele   SÜDTIROLEAN €
(☑0471 97 39 38; Via Goethe 3; meals €25; ⊙noon-4pm & 6-11pm) Dating back to 1277 and owned by the same family since 1840, this multi-level, antique-stuffed restaurant is well loved for its schnitzels and steaks along with local favourites risotto with rabbit *ragù* and rosemary, or jugged venison with polenta. There's some good vegetarian options and much of the produce is organic. The attached bar (⊙9am-1am) is pleasantly rowdy too.

★ Zur Kaiserkron   MODERN SÜDTIROLEAN €€
(☑0471 98 02 14; www.kaiserkron.bz; Piazza della Mostra 2; meals €45; ⊙noon-2.30pm & 7-9.30pm Mon-Sat) Refined but unfussy takes on regional favourites fill the menu at this calm and elegant dining room, and excellent produce is allowed to shine. It's tempting to just choose a selection from their interesting starters – say spelt ravioli with fresh curd cheese or mountain lentil soup with speck chips – but meaty mains are particuarly well executed.

♡ Drinking & Nightlife

Bolzano after dark may come as a surprise. The pristine city centre is often hushed at 8pm, but it's a different story around midnight. Follow the locals heading for Piazza delle Erbe's bar strip or the beer halls – including local Forst and the Bavarian Paulaner – along Via Argentieri and Via Goethe.

★ Enovit   WINE BAR
(Via Dott Streiter 30; ⊙10am-1pm & 3.30-8.30pm Mon-Fri, 10am-1pm Sat) An older, well-dressed

lot frequents this warm, woody corner bar and shop for expertly recommended, generously poured local wines by the glass. If there's a crowd – and on Fridays there *always* is – it kicks on past closing.

Temple Bar   IRISH PUB
(Piazza Domenicani 20; ⊙10.30am-1am Tue-Sat, 3pm-1am Sun & Mon) Tanya and Stephen's little slice of Dublin was recently awarded a coveted 'best Irish pub outside Ireland' title. While it's Irish to the core with welcoming staff, pints and big matches on the big screen, it's also quintessentially Bolzanino, with great *spritzes*, wine and a gang of hiking-, skiing- and sports-mad locals ready to offer up tips and advice.

Information

Hospital (☑0471 90 81 11; Via Böhler) Out of the centre of Bolzano towards Merano.

Police Station (☑0471 94 76 80, 0471 94 76 11; Via Marconi 33)

Tourist Office (☑0471 30 70 00; www.bolzano-bozen.it; Piazza Walther 8; ⊙9am-7pm Mon-Fri, 9.30am-6pm Sat)

Merano (Meran)

POP 38,200 / ELEV 325M

With its leafy boulevards, birdsong, oleanders and cacti, Merano feels like you've stumbled into a valley paradise. Long lauded for its sunny microclimate, this pretty town (and one-time Tyrolean capital) was a Habsburg-era spa and the hot destination of its day. The Jugendstil (art nouveau) villas, recuperative walks and the grand riverside Kurhaus fan out from its intact medieval core. The city's therapeutic traditions have served it well in the new millennium, with spa hotels drawing a new generation of health-conscious visitors and a booming organics movement in the surrounding valleys. German is spoken widely here, sausage and beer stalls dot the streets and an annual open-air play celebrates Napoleonic-era Tyrolean freedom fighter Andreas Hofer. Despite the palm trees, you're far closer to Vienna than Rome.

◉ Sights

★ Castel Trauttmansdorff   GARDENS
See p48.

Kunst Meran   ART GALLERY
(☑0473 21 26 43; www.kunstmeranoarte.org; Via Portici 16; adult/reduced €6/5; ⊙10am-6pm

Tue-Sun, 11am-7pm summer) Shows of high-profile international and regional artists are installed in this contemporary gallery, a thoughtful refiguring of a skinny medieval town house. Ask about their monthly talks over *aperitivo*.

🏃 Activities

Some 6km east of town, a cable car (Via Val di Nova; one way/return €13.50/18.50) carries winter-sports enthusiasts up to Piffing in Merano 2000 (www.hafling-meran2000.eu), with 30km of mostly beginner slopes. Bus 1B links Merano with the valley station. The tourist offices have details of the many other cable cars and lifts that ring the town, including the Falzeben gondola from Avelengo (Hafling) to Piffing (one way/return €10/15) and the chairlift (one way/return €4/5.50) from Merano to the village of Tirolo (Dorf Tirol). In summer, you can buy a 4-day Funicard (adult €48) for unlimited cable car and chairlift access.

★ Terme Merano   THERMAL BATHS
(☑0473 25 20 00; www.thermemeran.it; Piazza Terme 1; bathing pass 2hr/all day €12.50/18; ☺9am-10pm) Bolzano-born Matteo Thun's dream commission – a modern redevelopment of the town's thermal baths – was reopened in 2005. It houses 13 indoor pools and various saunas within a massive glass cube; there's another 12 outdoor pools open in summer. Swim through the sluice and be met by a vision of palm-studded gardens and snow-topped mountains beyond.

Don't forget to bring or rent a towel. The front desk can give first-timers a rundown on the potentially baffling change-room routine; see the website for details of the excellent wellness treatments available upstairs.

Promenades   WALKING
The promenade or *passeggiata* (evening stroll) has long been a Merano institution. Fin-de-siècle-era walks trace the river, traverse pretty parks and skirt Monte Benedetto (514m). A winter and summer pair follow opposing sides of the river, one shady, one sunny. The Gilfpromenade follows 24 poems carved on wooden benches (also handy for a breather). The lovely Tappeiner meanders above the town for 4km.

The tourist office offers guides in summer, or can give you a detailed map; all routes have helpful signage.

Castle Trauttmansdorff, Merano

🛏 Sleeping

Youth Hostel Merano   HOSTEL €
(☑0473 20 14 75; meran.jugendherberge.it; Via Carducci 77; dm/s €25.50/28; P@?🖶) A five-minute stroll from both the train station and the riverside promenade, this hostel is bright and modern, with a sunny terrace and other down-time extras. It has 59 beds, either singles or en suite dorms.

★ Ottmanngut   BOUTIQUE HOTEL €€
(☑0473 44 96 56; www.ottmanngut.it; Via Verdi 18; s/d €110/160; ?) 🍴 This boutique hotel encapsulates Merano's beguiling mix of stately sophistication, natural beauty and gently bohemian back story. The remodelled town house has nine rooms scattered over three floors, and is set among terraced vineyards a scant five-minute walk from the centre. Individually furnished, antique-strewn rooms evoke different moods, each highlighting the different landscape glimpsed from the window.

Multicourse breakfasts are a highlight, both because of the beautiful conservatory where they are served but also because of the care and attention with which they are prepared.

★ Miramonti   BOUTIQUE HOTEL €€€
(☑0473 27 93 35; www.hotel-miramonti.com; Via Santa Caterina 14, Avelengo; d €190-240; P✳🅿🖶) 🍴 This extraordinary small hotel, 15 minutes' drive from town, nestles on the

side of a mountain at 1230m. Rooms are vast, cosy and have awe-inspiring views – with such a potent mix, it's hard not to retreat entirely. But you'll be coaxed downstairs by the spa facilities, a sun terrace with lambskins and blankets, or a spot of 'forest therapy' in the nearby woods.

The glass-walled Panorama restaurant welcomes nonguests, and serves adventurous, beautifully presented dishes using local produce. The entire young team exemplify Südtirolean hospitality, relaxed but attentive to every detail.

🍴 Eating & Drinking

As befits a town dedicated to bodily pleasure, Merano has an excellent fine-dining scene, including the Michelin-starred Sissi and Castel Fragsburg. Via Portici brims with speck-dealing delis, *konditorei* line Corso della Libertà, and there are more late-night imbibing options, often squirreled down lanes, than you'd imagine.

★ Pur Südtirol   DELI, WINE BAR €

(www.pursuedtirol.com; Corso della Libertà 35; plates from €9; ⊙9am-7.30pm Mon-Fri, to 2pm Sat; ♨) This stylish regional showcase has an amazing selection of farm produce: wine, cider, some 80 varieties of cheese, speck and sausage, pastries and breads, tisanes and body care. Everything is hyperlocal (take Anton Oberhöller's chocolate, flavoured with apple, lemon balm or dark bread crisps).

Specially commissioned wood, glass and textiles fill one corner of the shop. Stay for a coffee, glass of wine or the *bretteljause* – a plate of cured meat – at one of the communal tables.

Sissi   GASTRONOMIC €€€

(☑0473 23 10 62; www.sissi.andreafenoglio.com; Via Galilei 44; meals €60, degustation €60-90) Andrea Fenoglio is one of the region's best-loved chefs and his big personality fills this small early-20th-century room. The food here is inventive, for sure, but the experience is warm and almost casual. Even the most experimental dish retains a connection to the traditional, or what Fenoglio calls 'memory food'.

Up to 20 wines are available by the glass, a pleasure if you're dining solo or just have a wide-roaming palette.

Café Kunsthaus   BAR

(Via Portici 16; ⊙8.30am-8pm Mon-Thu, to 1am Fri & Sat, 10am-6pm Sun) You can while away the hours in this relaxed gallery cafe, then find yourself still here when the DJs begin and the beer and pizzas are doing the rounds. Note: evening access is from the back lane off Via Risparmio.

❶ Information

Ospedale Merano (☑0473 26 33 33; Via Rossini 5) For medical emergencies.

Tourist Office (☑0473 23 52 23; www.meran info.it; Corso Libertà 35; ⊙9am-6pm Mon-Fri, to 4pm Sat, 10am-12.30pm Sun summer, 9am-12.30pm & 2-5pm Mon-Fri, 9.30am-12.30pm Sat winter)

WORTH A TRIP

WINE TASTING TRAIL
···

Follow Alto Adige's Weinstraße (wine road) far enough south from Bolzano and you'll hit **Paradeis** (Alois Lageder; ☑0471 80 95 80; www.aloislageder.eu/paradeis; Piazza Geltrude 5, Magrè; meals €40-65; ⊙10am-8pm, dining room noon-4pm Mon-Sat, to 11pm Thu). Take a seat at the long communal table, crafted from the wood of a 250-year-old oak tree, at fourth-generation winemaker Alois Lageder's biodynamic *weinschenke/vineria* (winery), and start tasting. Book for lunch in the stunning dining room or linger over a bottle and plate of cheese in the pretty courtyard. Whites – highly finessed, Germanic in style, but shot through with the warmth and verve of an Italian summer – are the money here; over 70% of production is devoted to pinot grigio, chardonnay and Gewürztraminer. Even so, Lageder's pinot noir and local Lagrein are highly regarded.

If you're up for more tasting, or just a pleasant day's cycle, the Weinstraße begins northwest of Bolzano in Nals, meanders past Terlano (Terlan) through Upper Adige (Überetsch) and Lower Adige (Unterland) until it reaches Salorno (Salurn). Native grape varieties line the route: Lagrein, Vernatsch and local varietal Gewürztraminer, along with well-adapted imports pinot blanc, sauvignon, merlot and cabernet. For details of cellar doors, accommodation and bike trails, see www.weinstrasse.com.

Valtellina

From the north end of Lake Como, the Valtellina cuts a broad swathe of a valley (at whose centre runs the Adda river) eastward between the Swiss mountain frontier to the north and the Orobie Alps to the south. Much of its steep, northern flank is carpeted by the vineyards (mostly the *nebbiolo* grape variety) that produce such coveted drops as Sforzato (Sfurzat). You can largely skip the valley towns, but a detour to the hillside wine villages is worthwhile. Two points of reference are Ponte, 8km east of Sondrio, and Teglio (with a cute Romanesque church), 8km further east. The brisk climb up among the vineyards affords sweeping views across the valley. And what better way to taste Valtellina reds than by calling into any local trattoria?

✖ Eating

Altavilla   CHALET RESTAURANT €€

(☑ 0342 72 03 55; www.altavilla.info; Via ai Monti 46, Bianzone; meals €30; ☺ noon-2.30pm & 7-10pm Tue-Sun, daily Aug; P 🛜 🖩) Located in the heart of the Valtellina's finest vineyards in Bianzone, just north of Teglio, is Altavilla, Anna Bertola's charming Alpine chalet and restaurant, one of the gastronomic treats of the region. Expect expert wine recommendations to accompany traditional mountain dishes such as *sciàtt* (buckwheat pancakes stuffed with Bitto cheese) and *pizzocheri* buckwheat pasta. The artisanal salami, mountain venison and aged Bitto cheese are particular highlights, as is the 500-label wine list.

Reserve a room (singles €25 to €42, doubles €42 to €68) for the night so you can sleep it off afterwards.

Osteria del Crotto   OSTERIA €€

(☑ 0342 61 48 00; www.osteriadelcrotto.it; Via Pedemontana 22; meals €25-35) Osteria del Crotto serves a whole slew of Slow Food Movement–authenticated products such as *violino di capra della Valchiavenna* (literally 'violin goat of the Valchiavenna'), a traditional salami made from the shank, which is sliced by resting it on the shoulder and shaving it as a violin player moves his bow.

ℹ Information

Valtellina Tourist Office (☑ 0342 45 11 50; www.valtellina.it; Piazzale Bertacchi 77, Sondrio; ☺ 9am-12.30pm & 3.30-6.30pm Mon-Fri, 9am-noon Sat)

Parco Nazionale dello Stelvio

It's not quite Yellowstone, but 1346-sq-km Parco Nazionale dello Stelvio (☑ 0473 83 04 30; www.parks.it/parco.nazionale.stelvio) FREE is the Alps' largest national park, spilling into the next-door region of Lombardy and bordering Switzerland's Parco Nazionale Svizzero. It's primarily the preserve of walkers who come for the extensive network of well-organised mountain huts and marked trails that, while often challenging, don't require the mountaineering skills necessary elsewhere in the Dolomites. Stelvio's central massif is guarded over by Monte Cevedale (3769m) and Ortles (3905m), protecting glaciers, forests and numerous wildlife species, not to mention many mountain traditions and histories.

Ski facilities are rare, but Stelvio has a couple of well-serviced runs at Solda and the Passo dello Stelvio (2757m), both of which offer the novelty of year-round skiing. The latter is the second-highest pass in the Alps and is approached from the north from the hamlet of Trafoi (1543m) on one of Europe's most spectacular roads, a series of tight switchbacks covering 15km, with some very steep gradients. The road is also famous among cyclists, who train all winter to prepare for its gut-wrenching ascent, and often features in the Giro d'Italia. The hair-raising high pass is only open from June to September, and is subject to closures dependent on early or late snowfall.

ROAD TRIP ESSENTIALS

Italy
Driving Guide

Italy's stunning natural scenery, comprehensive road network and passion for cars make it a wonderful road-trip destination.

Driving Fast Facts

→ **Right or left?** Drive on the right
→ **Manual or automatic?** Mostly manual
→ **Legal driving age** 18
→ **Top speed limit** 130km/h to 150km/h (on autostradas)
→ **Signature car** Flaming red Ferrari or Fiat 500

DRIVING LICENCE & DOCUMENTS

When driving in Italy you are required to carry with you:

→ The vehicle registration document
→ Your driving licence
→ Proof of third-party liability insurance

Driving Licence

→ All EU member states' driving licences are fully recognised throughout Europe.
→ Travellers from other countries should obtain an International Driving Permit (IDP) through their national automobile association. This should be carried with your licence; it is not a substitute for it.
→ No licence is needed to ride a scooter under 50cc. To ride a motorcycle or scooter up to 125cc, you'll need a licence (a car licence will do). For motorcycles over 125cc you need a motorcycle licence.

INSURANCE

→ Third-party liability insurance is mandatory for all vehicles in Italy, including cars brought in from abroad.
→ If driving an EU-registered vehicle, your home country insurance is sufficient. Ask your insurer for a European Accident Statement (EAS) form, which can simplify matters in the event of an accident.
→ Hire agencies provide the minimum legal insurance, but you can supplement it if you choose.

HIRING A CAR

Car-hire agencies are widespread in Italy but pre-booking on the internet is often cheaper. Considerations before renting:

→ Bear in mind that a car is generally more hassle than it's worth in cities, so only hire one for the time you'll be on the open road.
→ Consider vehicle size carefully. High fuel prices, extremely narrow streets and tight parking conditions mean that smaller is often better.
→ Road signs can be iffy in remote areas, so consider booking and paying for satnav.

Standard regulations:

→ Many agencies have a minimum rental age of 25 and a maximum of 79. You can sometimes hire if you're over 21 but supplementary costs will apply.

Road Distances (km)

Note

Distances between Palermo and mainland towns do not take into account the ferry from Reggio di Calabria to Messina. Add an extra hour to your journey time to allow for this crossing.

	Bari	Bologna	Florence	Genoa	Milan	Naples	Palermo	Perugia	Reggio di Calabria	Rome	Siena	Trento	Trieste	Turin	Venice
Bologna	681														
Florence	784	106													
Genoa	996	285	268												
Milan	899	218	324	156											
Naples	322	640	534	758	858										
Palermo	734	1415	1345	1569	1633	811									
Perugia	612	270	164	432	488	408	1219								
Reggio di Calabria	490	1171	1101	1325	1389	567	272	816							
Rome	482	408	302	526	626	232	1043	170	664						
Siena	714	176	70	296	394	464	1275	103	867	232					
Trento	892	233	339	341	218	874	1626	459	1222	641	375				
Trieste	995	308	414	336	420	948	1689	543	1445	715	484	279			
Turin	1019	338	442	174	139	932	1743	545	1307	702	460	349	551		
Venice	806	269	265	387	284	899	799	394	1296	567	335	167	165	415	
Verona	808	141	247	282	164	781	1534	377	1139	549	293	97	250	295	120

➡ To rent you'll need a credit card, valid driver's licence (with IDP if necessary) and passport or photo ID. Note that some companies require that you've had your licence for at least a year.

➡ Hire cars come with the minimum legal insurance, which you can supplement by purchasing additional coverage.

➡ Check with your credit-card company to see if it offers a Collision Damage Waiver, which covers you for additional damage if you use that card to pay for the car.

The following are among the most competitive multinational and Italian car-hire agencies.

Avis (☎199 100133; www.avis.com)
Budget (☎800 4723325; www.budget.com)
Europcar (☎199 307030; www.europcar.com)
Hertz (☎199 112211; www.hertz.com)
Italy by Car (☎091 6393120; www.italybycar.it) Partners with Thrifty.
Maggiore (☎199 151120; www.maggiore.it) Partners with Alamo and National.

Motorcycles

Agencies throughout Italy rent motorbikes, ranging from small Vespas to larger touring bikes. Prices start at around €80/400 per day/week for a 650cc motorcycle.

BRINGING YOUR OWN VEHICLE

There are no major obstacles to driving your own vehicle into Italy. But you will have to adjust your car's headlights if it's a left-hand-drive UK model. You'll need to carry the following in the car:

➡ A warning triangle
➡ A fluorescent reflective vest to wear if you have to stop on a major road
➡ Snow chains if travelling in mountainous areas between 15 October and 15 April

MAPS

We recommend you purchase a good road map for your trip. The best driving maps are produced by the **Touring Club Italiano** (www.touringclub.com), Italy's largest map publisher. They are available at bookstores across Italy or online at the following:

Omni Resources (www.omnimap.com)

Stanfords (www.stanfords.co.uk)

ROADS & CONDITIONS

Italy's extensive road network covers the entire peninsula and with enough patience you'll be able to get just about anywhere. Road quality varies – the autostradas are generally excellent but smaller roads, particularly in rural areas, are not always great. Heavy rain can cause axle-busting potholes to form and road surfaces to crumble.

Traffic in and around the main cities is bad during morning and evening rush hours. Coastal roads get very busy on summer weekends. As a rule, traffic is quietest between 2pm and 4pm.

Road Categories

Autostradas Italy boasts an extensive network of autostradas, represented on road signs by a white 'A' followed by a number on a green background. The main north–south link is the Autostrada del Sole (the 'Motorway of the Sun'), which runs from Milan (Milano) to Reggio di Calabria. It's called the A1 from Milan to Rome (Roma), the A2 from Rome to Naples (Napoli), and the A3 from Naples to Reggio di Calabria. There are tolls on most motorways, payable by cash or credit card as you exit. To calculate the toll price for any given journey, use the route planner on www.autostrade.it.

Strade statali State highways; represented on maps by 'S' or 'SS'. Vary from four-lane highways to two-lane main roads. The latter can be extremely slow, especially in mountainous regions.

Strade regionali Regional highways connecting small villages. Coded 'SR' or 'R'.

Strade provinciali Provincial highways; coded 'SP' or 'P'.

Strade locali Often not even paved or mapped.

Along with their A or SS number, some Italian roads are labelled with an E number – for example, the A4 autostrada is also shown as the E64 on maps and signs. This E number refers to the road's designation on the Europe-wide E-road network. E routes, which often cross national boundaries, are generally made up of major national roads strung together. The E70, for example, traverses 10 countries and includes the Italian A4, A21 and A32 autostradas, as it runs from northern Spain to Georgia.

Limited Traffic Zones

Many town and city centres are off-limits to unauthorised traffic at certain times. If you drive past a sign with the wording *Zona a Traffico Limitato* you are entering a Limited Traffic Zone (ZTL) and risk being caught on camera and fined. Being in a hire car will not exempt you from this rule.

If you think your hotel might be in a ZTL, contact them beforehand to ask about access arrangements.

ROAD RULES

➡ Drive on the right side of the road and overtake on the left. Unless otherwise indicated, give way to cars entering an intersection from a road on your right.

➡ Seatbelt use (front and rear) is required by law; violators are subject to an on-the-spot fine.

➡ In the event of a breakdown, a warning triangle is compulsory, as is use of an approved yellow or orange safety vest if you leave your

Road-Trip Websites

AUTOMOBILE ASSOCIATIONS

Automobile Club d'Italia (www.aci.it) Has a comprehensive online guide to motoring in Italy. Provides 24-hour roadside assistance.

CONDITIONS & TRAFFIC

Autostrade (www.autostrade.it) Route planner, weather forecasts and the traffic situation in real time. Also lists service stations, petrol prices and toll costs.

MAPS

Michelin (www.viamichelin.it) Online road-trip planner.

Tutto Città (www.tuttocitta.it) Good for detailed town and city maps.

Driving Problem-Buster

I can't speak Italian, will that be a problem? When at a petrol station you might have to ask the attendant for your fill-up. The thing to do here is ask for the amount you want, so *venti euro* for €20 or *pieno* for full. And always specify *benzina senza piombo* for unleaded petrol and *gasolio* for diesel. At autostrada toll booths, the amount you owe appears on a read-out by the booth.

What should I do if my car breaks down? Call the service number of your car-hire company. The Automobile Club d'Italia (ACI) provides a 24-hour roadside emergency service – call ☎803 116 from a landline or mobile with an Italian provider or ☎800 116800 from a foreign mobile phone. Foreigners do not have to join but instead pay a per-incident fee. Note that in the event of a breakdown, a warning triangle is compulsory, as is use of an approved yellow or orange safety vest if you leave your vehicle.

What if I have an accident? For minor accidents there's no need to call the police. Fill in an accident report – Constatazione Amichevole di Incidente (CAI; Agreed Motor Accident Statement) – through your car-hire firm or insurance company.

What should I do if I get stopped by the police? The police will want to see your passport (or photo ID), licence, car registration papers and proof of insurance.

What if I can't find anywhere to stay? Always book ahead in summer and popular holiday periods. Italy doesn't have chains of roadside motels so if it's getting late head to the nearest town and look for signs for an *albergo* (hotel).

Will I be able to find ATMs? Some autostrada service stations have ATMs (known as *bancomat* in Italian). Otherwise, they are widely available in towns and cities.

Will I need to pay tolls in advance? No. When you join an autostrada you have to pick up a ticket at the barrier. When you exit you pay based on the distance you've covered. Pay by cash or credit card. Avoid Telepass lanes at toll stations.

Are the road signs easy to read? Most signs are fairly obvious but it helps to know that town/city centres are indicated by the word *centro* and a kind of black-and-white bullseye sign; *divieto fermata* means 'no stopping'; and *tutte le direzione* means 'all directions'.

vehicle. Recommended accessories include a first-aid kit, spare-bulb kit and fire extinguisher.

➡ Italy's blood-alcohol limit is 0.05%, and random breath tests take place. If you're involved in an accident while under the influence, the penalties can be severe.

➡ Headlights are compulsory day and night for all vehicles on autostradas and main roads.

➡ Helmets are required on all two-wheeled transport.

➡ Motorbikes can enter most restricted traffic areas in Italian cities.

➡ Speeding fines follow EU standards and are proportionate with the number of kilometres that you are caught driving over the speed limit, reaching up to €2000 with possible suspension of your driving licence. Speed limits are as follows:

Autostradas 130km/h to 150km/h
Other main highways 110km/h
Minor, non-urban roads 90km/h
Built-up areas 50km/h

Road Etiquette

➡ Italian drivers are fast, aggressive and skilful. Lane hopping and late braking are the norm and it's not uncommon to see cars tailgating at 130km/h. Don't expect cars to slow down for you or let you out. As soon as you see a gap, go for it. Italians expect the unexpected and react swiftly, but they're not used to ditherers, so be decisive.

➡ Flashing is common on the roads and has several meanings. If a car behind you flashes it means: 'Get out of the way' or 'Don't pull out, I'm not stopping'. But if an approaching car flashes you, it's warning you that there's a police check ahead.

➡ Use of the car horn is widespread. It might be a warning but it might equally be an expression of frustration at slow-moving traffic or celebration that the traffic light's turning green.

PARKING

➡ Parking is a major headache. Space is at a premium in towns and cities and Italy's traffic wardens are annoyingly efficient.

➡ Parking spaces outlined in blue are designated for paid parking – get a ticket from the nearest meter (coins only) or *tabaccaio* (tobacconist) and display it on your dashboard. Note, however, that charges often don't apply overnight, typically between 8pm and 8am.

Coins

Always try to keep some coins to hand. They come in very useful for parking meters.

➡ White or yellow lines almost always indicate that residential permits are needed.

➡ Traffic police generally turn a blind eye to motorcycles or scooters parked on footpaths.

FUEL

➡ You'll find filling stations all over, but smaller ones tend to close between about 1pm and 3.30pm and on Sunday afternoons.

➡ Many have *fai da te* (self-service) pumps that you can use any time. Simply insert a bank note into the payment machine and press the number of the pump you want.

➡ Italy's petrol prices are among the highest in Europe and vary from one service station *(benzinaio, stazione di servizio)* to another. When this book was researched, lead-free petrol *(benzina senza piombo)* averaged €1.93 per litre, with diesel *(gasolio)* averaging €1.81 per litre.

Local Expert: Driving Tips

A representative of the Automobile Club d'Italia (ACI) offers these pearls to ease your way on Italian roads:

➡ Pay particular attention to the weather. In summer when it gets very hot, always carry a bottle of water with you and have some fresh fruit to eat. Italy is a sunny country but, in winter, watch out for ice, snow and fog.

➡ On the extra-urban roads and autostradas, cars have to have their headlights on even during the day.

➡ Watch out for signs at the autostrada toll booths – the lanes marked 'Telepass' are for cars that pay through an automatic electronic system without stopping.

➡ Watch out in the cities – big and small – for the Limited Traffic Zones (ZTL) and pay parking. There is no universal system for indicating these or their hours.

Italy Playlist

Nessun Dorma Puccini

O sole mio Traditional

Tu vuoi fare l'americano Renato Carsone

Vieni via con me Paolo Conte

That's Amore Dean Martin

Four Seasons Vivaldi

SAFETY

The main safety threat to motorists is theft. Hire cars and foreign vehicles are a target for robbers and although you're unlikely to have a problem, thefts do occur. As a general rule, always lock your car and never leave anything showing, particularly valuables, and certainly not overnight. If at all possible, avoid leaving luggage in an unattended car. It's a good idea to pay extra to leave your car in supervised car parks.

RADIO

RAI, Italy's state broadcaster, operates three national radio stations – Radio 1, 2 and 3 – offering news, current affairs, classical and commercial music, and endless phone-ins. Isoradio, another RAI station, provides regular news and traffic bulletins. There are also thousands of commercial radio stations, many broadcasting locally. Major ones include Radio Capital, good for modern hits; Radio Deejay, aimed at a younger audience; and Radio 24, which airs news and talk shows.

Italy Travel Guide

GETTING THERE & AWAY

AIR

Italy's main international airports:

Rome Leonardo da Vinci (Fiumicino; www.adr.it) Italy's principal airport.

Rome Ciampino (www.adr.it) Hub for Ryanair flights to Rome (Roma).

Milan Malpensa (www.milanomalpensa1.eu, www.milanomalpensa2.eu) Main airport of Milan (Milano).

Milan Linate (www.milanolinate.eu) Milan's second airport.

Bergamo Orio al Serio (www.sacbo.it)

Turin (www.turin-airport.com)

Bologna Guglielmo Marconi (www.bologna-airport.it)

Pisa Galileo Galilei (www.pisa-airport.com) Main international airport for Tuscany.

Venice Marco Polo (www.veniceairport.it)

Naples Capodichino (www.gesac.it)

Bari Palese (www.aeroportidipuglia.it)

Catania Fontanarossa (www.aeroporto.catania.it) Sicily's busiest airport.

Palermo Falcone-Borsellino (www.gesap.it)

Cagliari Elmas (www.sogaer.it) Main gateway for Sardinia.

Car hire is available at all of these airports.

CAR & MOTORCYCLE

Driving into Italy is fairly straightforward – thanks to the Schengen Agreement, there are no customs checks when driving in from neighbours France, Switzerland, Austria and Slovenia.

Aside from the coast roads linking Italy with France and Slovenia, border crossings into Italy mostly involve tunnels through the Alps (open year-round) or mountain passes (seasonally closed or requiring snow chains). The list below outlines the major points of entry.

Austria From Innsbruck to Bolzano via A22/E45 (Brenner Pass); Villach to Tarvisio via A23/E55.

France From Nice to Ventimiglia via A10/E80; Modane to Turin (Torino) via A32/E70 (Fréjus Tunnel); Chamonix to Courmayeur via A5/E25 (Mont Blanc Tunnel).

Slovenia From Sežana to Trieste via SS58/E70.

Switzerland From Martigny to Aosta via SS27/E27 (Grand St Bernard Tunnel); Lugano to Como via A9/E35.

SEA

International car ferries sail to Italy from Albania, Croatia, Greece, Malta, Montenegro, Morocco, Slovenia, Spain and Tunisia. Some routes only operate in summer, when ticket prices rise. Prices for vehicles vary according to their size. Car hire is not always available at ports, so check beforehand on the nearest agency.

The website www.traghettionline.com (in Italian) details all of the ferry companies in the Mediterranean. The principal operators serving Italy:

Agoudimos Lines (www.agoudimos.it) Greece to Bari (11 to 16 hours) and Brindisi (seven to 14 hours).

Endeavor Lines (www.endeavor-lines.com) Greece to Brindisi (seven to 14 hours).

Grandi Navi Veloci (www.gnv.it) Barcelona to Genoa (18 hours).

Jadrolinija (www.jadrolinija.hr) Croatia to Ancona (from nine hours) and Bari (10 hours).

Practicalities

➜ **Smoking** Banned in all closed public spaces.

➜ **Time** Italy uses the 24-hour clock and is on Central European Time, one hour ahead of GMT/UTC.

➜ **TV & DVD** The main TV channels: state-run RAI-1, RAI-2 and RAI-3; Canale 5, Italia 1 and Rete 4; and La 7. Italian DVDs are regionally coded 2.

➜ **Weights & Measures** Italy uses the metric system, so kilometres not miles, litres not gallons.

Minoan Lines (www.minoan.gr) Greece to Venice (22 to 30 hours) and Ancona (16 to 22 hours).

Montenegro Lines (www.montenegrolines. net) Bar to Bari (nine hours).

Superfast (www.superfast.com) Greece to Bari (11 to 16 hours) and Ancona (16 to 22 hours).

Ventouris (www.ventouris.gr) Albania to Bari (eight hours).

TRAIN

Regular trains on two western lines connect Italy with France (one along the coast and the other from Turin into the French Alps). Trains from Milan head north into Switzerland and on towards the Benelux countries. Further east, two lines connect with Central and Eastern Europe.

Trenitalia (www.trenitalia.com) offers various train and car-hire packages that allow you to save on hire charges when you book a train ticket – see the website for details.

DIRECTORY A–Z

ACCOMMODATION

From dreamy villas to chic boutique hotels, historic hideaways and ravishing farmstays, Italy offers accommodation to suit every taste and budget.

Seasons & Rates

➜ Hotel rates fluctuate enormously from high to low season, and even from day to day depending on demand, season and booking method (online, through an agency etc).

➜ As a rule, peak rates apply at Easter, in summer and over the Christmas/New Year period. But there are exceptions – in the mountains, high season means the ski season (December to late March). Also, August is high season on the coast but low season in many cities where hotels offer discounts.

➜ Southern Italy is generally cheaper than the north.

Reservations

➜ Always book ahead in peak season, even if it's only for the first night or two.

➜ In the off-season, it always pays to call ahead to check that your hotel is open. Many coastal hotels close for winter, typically opening from late March to late October.

➜ Hotels usually require that reservations be confirmed with a credit-card number. No-shows will be docked a night's accommodation.

B&Bs

B&Bs can be found throughout the country in both urban and rural settings. Options include restored farmhouses, city *palazzi* (mansions), seaside bungalows and rooms in family houses. Prices vary but as a rule B&Bs are often better value than hotels in the same category. Note that breakfast in an Italian B&B will often be a continental combination of bread rolls, croissants, ham and cheese. For more information, contact **Bed & Breakfast Italia** (www.bbitalia.it).

Hotels & Pensioni

A *pensione* is a small, family-run hotel or guesthouse. Hotels are bigger and more expensive than *pensioni*, although at the cheaper end of the market, there's often little difference between the two. All hotels are rated from one to five stars, although this rating relates to facilities only and

Sleeping Price Ranges

The price ranges listed in this book refer to a double room with bathroom.

€ less than €100

€€ €100–200

€€€ more than €200

gives no indication of value, comfort, atmosphere or friendliness.

Breakfast in cheaper hotels is rarely worth setting the alarm for. If you have the option, save your money and pop into a bar for a coffee and *cornetto* (croissant).

➡ One-star hotels and *pensioni* tend to be basic and often do not offer private bathrooms.

➡ Two-star places are similar but rooms will generally have a private bathroom.

➡ Three-star hotel rooms will come with a hairdryer, minibar (or fridge), safe and air-con. Many will also have satellite TV and wi-fi.

➡ Four- and five-star hotels offer facilities such as room service, laundry and dry-cleaning.

Agriturismi

From rustic country houses to luxurious estates and fully functioning farms, Italian farmstays, known as *agriturismi* (singular – *agriturismo*) are hugely popular. Comfort levels, facilities and prices vary accordingly but the best will offer swimming pools and top-class accommodation. Many also operate restaurants specialising in traditional local cuisine.

Agriturismi have long thrived in Tuscany and Umbria, but you'll now find them across the country. For listings and further details, check out the following sites:

Agritour (www.agritour.net)

Agriturismo.com (www.agriturismo.com)

Agriturismo.it (www.agriturismo.it)

Agriturismo-Italia.net (www.agriturismo-italia.net)

Agriturismo.net (www.agriturismo.net)

Agriturismo Vero (www.agriturismovero.com)

Agriturist (www.agriturist.com)

Other Options

Camping A popular summer option. Most campsites are big, summer-only complexes with swimming pools, restaurants and supermarkets. Many have space for RVs and offer bungalows or simple, self-contained flats. Minimum stays sometimes apply in high season. Check out www.campeggi.com and www.camping.it.

Hostels Hostels around the country offer dorm beds and private rooms. Breakfast is usually included in rates and dinner is sometimes available for about €10. For listings and further details, see www.aighostels.com or www.hostelworld.com.

Book Your Stay Online

For more accommodation reviews by Lonely Planet authors, check out http://hotels.lonelyplanet.com/italy. You'll find independent reviews, as well as recommendations on the best places to stay. Best of all, you can book online.

Convents & Monasteries Some convents and monasteries provide basic accommodation. Expect curfews, few frills and value for money. Useful resources include www.monasterystays.com, www.initaly.com/agri/convents.htm and www.santasusanna.org/comingToRome/convents.html.

Refuges Mountain huts kitted out with bunk rooms sleeping anything from two to a dozen or more people. Many offer half-board (bed, breakfast and dinner) and most are open from mid-June to mid-September.

Villas Villas and *fattorie* (farmhouses) can be rented in their entirety or sometimes by the room. Many have swimming pools.

ELECTRICITY

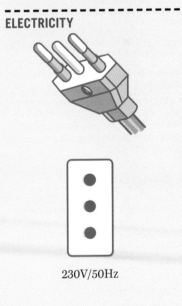

230V/50Hz

120V/60Hz

FOOD

A full Italian meal consists of an antipasto (appetiser), *primo* (first course, usually a pasta, risotto or polenta), *secondo* (second course, meat or fish) with *contorno* (vegetable side dish) or *insalata* (salad), and *dolce* (dessert) and/or fruit. When eating out it's perfectly OK to mix and match and order, say, a *primo* followed by an *insalata* or *contorno*.

Where to Eat

Trattorias Traditional, often family-run eateries offering simple, local food and wine. Some newer-wave trattorias offer more creative fare and scholarly wine lists. Generally cheap to midrange in price.

Eating Price Ranges

The following price ranges refer to a meal consisting of a *primo* (first course), *secondo* (second course), *dolce* (dessert) and a glass of house wine for one:

€ less than €25

€€ €25–45

€€€ more than €45

Restaurants More formal, and more expensive, than trattorias, with more choice and smarter service. Reservations are generally required for popular and top-end places.

Pizzerias Alongside pizza, many pizzerias also offer antipasti, pastas, meat and vegetable dishes. They're often only open in the evening. The best have a wood-oven *(forno a legna)*.

Bars & Cafes Italians often breakfast on *cornetti* and coffee at a bar or cafe. Many bars and cafes sell *panini* (bread rolls with simple fillings) at lunchtime and serve a hot and cold buffet during the early evening *aperitivo* (aperitif) hour.

Wine Bars At an *enoteca* (plural – *enoteche*) you can drink wine by the glass and eat snacks such as cheeses, cold meats, bruschette and *crostini* (little toasts). Some also serve hot dishes.

Markets Most towns and cities have morning produce markets where you can stock up on picnic provisions. Villages might have a weekly market.

GAY & LESBIAN TRAVELLERS

➡ Homosexuality is legal in Italy and well tolerated in the major cities. However, overt displays of affection by homosexual couples could attract a negative response, particularly in the more conservative south and in smaller towns.

➡ There are gay clubs in Rome, Milan and Bologna, and a handful in places such as Florence (Firenze). Some coastal towns and resorts (such as Viareggio in Tuscany and Taormina in Sicily) see much more action in summer.

Useful resources:

Arcigay & Arcilesbica (www.arcigay.it) Bologna-based national organisation for gays and lesbians.

GayFriendlyItaly.com (www.gayfriendly italy.com) English-language site produced by Gay.it, with information on everything from hotels to homophobia issues and the law.

Gay.it (www.gay.it) Website listing gay bars and hotels across the country.

Pride (www.prideonline.it) National monthly magazine of art, music, politics and gay culture.

HEALTH

➡ Italy has a public health system that is legally bound to provide emergency care to everyone.

➡ EU nationals are entitled to reduced-cost, sometimes free, medical care with a European Health Insurance Card (EHIC), available from your home health authority.

➡ Non-EU citizens should take out medical insurance.

➡ For emergency treatment, you can go to the *pronto soccorso* (casualty) section of an *ospedale* (public hospital), though be prepared for a long wait.

➡ Pharmacists can give advice and sell over-the-counter medication for minor illnesses. Pharmacies generally keep the same hours as other shops, closing at night and on Sundays. A handful remain open on a rotation basis *(farmacie di turno)* for emergency purposes. These are usually listed in newspapers. Closed pharmacies display a list of the nearest ones open.

➡ In major cities you are likely to find English-speaking doctors or a translator service available.

➡ Italian tap water is fine to drink.

➡ No vaccinations are required for travel to Italy.

INTERNET ACCESS

➡ An increasing number of hotels, B&Bs, hostels and even *agriturismi* offer free wi-fi. You'll also find it in many bars and cafes.

➡ The 🛜 icon used throughout this book indicates wi-fi is available.

➡ Rome and Bologna are among the cities that provide free wi-fi, although you'll have to register for the service at www.romawireless.com (Rome) and www.comune.bologna.it/wireless (Bologna) and have an Italian mobile phone number.

➡ Venice (Venezia) offers pay-for wi-fi packages online at www.veniceconnected.com.

➡ Internet access is not as widespread in rural and southern Italy as in urban and northern areas.

➡ Internet cafes are thin on the ground. Typical charges range from €2 to €6 per hour. They might require formal photo ID.

➡ Many top-end hotels charge upwards of €10 per day for access.

MONEY

Italy uses the euro. Euro notes come in denominations of €500, €200, €100, €50, €20, €10 and €5; coins come in denominations of €2 and €1, and 50, 20, 10, five, two and one cents.

For the latest exchange rates, check out www.xe.com.

Admission Prices

➡ There are no hard and fast rules, but many state museums and galleries offer discounted admission to EU seniors and students.

➡ Typically, EU citizens under 18 and over 65 enter free and those aged between 18 and 24 pay a reduced rate.

➡ EU teachers might also qualify for concessions. In all cases you'll need photo ID to claim reduced entry.

ATMs

ATMs (known as *bancomat*) are widely available throughout Italy and are the best way to obtain local currency.

Credit Cards

➡ International credit and debit cards can be used in any ATM displaying the appropriate sign. Visa and MasterCard are among the most widely recognised, but others such as Cirrus and Maestro are also well covered.

Italian Wine Classifications

Italian wines are classified according to strict quality-control standards and carry one of four denominations:

DOCG (Denominazione di Origine Controllata e Garantita) Italy's best wines; made in specific areas according to stringent production rules.

DOC (Denominazione di Origine Controllata) Quality wines produced in defined regional areas.

IGT (Indicazione geografica tipica) Wines typical of a certain region.

VdT (Vino da Tavola) Wines for everyday drinking; often served as house wine in trattorias.

➜ Only some banks give cash advances over the counter, so you're better off using ATMs.

➜ Cards are good for paying in most hotels, restaurants, shops, supermarkets and toll booths. Some cheaper *pensioni*, trattorias and pizzerias only accept cash. Don't rely on credit cards at museums or galleries.

➜ Check any charges with your bank. Most banks now build a fee of around 2.75% into every foreign transaction. Also, ATM withdrawals can attract a further fee, usually around 1.5%.

➜ In an emergency, call to have your card blocked:

Amex (✆06 7290 0347 or your national call number)

Diners Club (✆800 393939)

MasterCard (✆800 870866)

Visa (✆800 819014)

Moneychangers

You can change money in banks, at post offices or at a *cambio* (exchange office). Post offices and banks tend to offer the best rates; exchange offices keep longer hours, but watch for high commissions and inferior rates.

OPENING HOURS

Banks 8.30am to 1.30pm and 2.45pm to 4.30pm Monday to Friday.

Bars & Cafes 7.30am to 8pm, sometimes until 1am or 2am.

Clubs 10pm to 4am.

Post Offices Main offices 8am to 7pm Monday to Friday, 8.30am to noon Saturday; branches 8am to 2pm weekdays, 8.30am to noon Saturday.

Tipping Guide

Taxis Round the fare up to the nearest euro.

Restaurants Many locals don't tip waiters, but most visitors leave 10% if there's no service charge.

Cafes Leave a coin (as little as €0.10 is acceptable) if you drank your coffee at the counter, or 10% if you sat at a table.

Hotels Bellhops usually expect €1 to €2 per bag; it's not necessary to tip the concierge, cleaners or front-desk staff.

Restaurants Noon to 3pm and 7.30pm to 11pm; sometimes later in summer and in the south. Kitchens often shut an hour earlier than final closing time; most places close at least one day a week.

Shops 9am to 1pm and 3.30pm to 7.30pm (or 4pm to 8pm) weekdays. In larger cities, department stores and supermarkets typically open 9am to 7.30pm or 10am to 8pm Monday to Saturday, some also on Sunday.

PUBLIC HOLIDAYS

Individual towns have public holidays to celebrate the feasts of their patron saints. National public holidays:

Capodanno (New Year's Day) 1 January

Epifania (Epiphany) 6 January

Pasquetta (Easter Monday) March/April

Giorno della Liberazione (Liberation Day) 25 April

Festa del Lavoro (Labour Day) 1 May

Festa della Repubblica (Republic Day) 2 June

Festa dei Santi Pietro e Paolo (Feast of St Peter & St Paul) 29 June

Ferragosto (Feast of the Assumption) 15 August

Festa di Ognisanti (All Saints' Day) 1 November

Festa dell'Immacolata Concezione (Feast of the Immaculate Conception) 8 December

Natale (Christmas Day) 25 December

Festa di Santo Stefano (Boxing Day) 26 December

SAFE TRAVEL

Italy is a safe country but petty theft can be a problem. There's no need for paranoia but be aware that thieves and pickpockets operate in touristy areas, so watch out when exploring the sights in Rome, Florence, Venice, Naples (Napoli) etc.

Cars, particularly those with foreign number plates or rental-company stickers, provide rich pickings for thieves – see p119.

In case of theft or loss, report the incident to the police within 24 hours and ask for a statement. Some tips:

➜ Keep essentials in a money belt but carry your day's spending money in a separate wallet.

→ Wear your bag/camera strap across your body and away from the road – thieves on mopeds can swipe a bag and be gone in seconds.

→ Never drape your bag over an empty chair at a street-side cafe or put it where you can't see it.

→ Always check your change to see you haven't been short changed.

TELEPHONE

Domestic Calls

→ Italian telephone area codes all begin with 0 and consist of up to four digits. Area codes are an integral part of all Italian phone numbers and must be dialled even when calling locally.

→ Mobile-phone numbers are nine or 10 digits and have a three-digit prefix starting with a 3.

→ Toll-free (free-phone) numbers are known as *numeri verdi* and usually start with 800.

→ Non-geographical numbers start with 840, 841, 848, 892, 899, 163, 166 or 199. Some six-digit national rate numbers are also in use (such as those for Alitalia, rail and postal information).

International Calls

→ To call Italy from abroad, call the international access number (☑011 in the USA, ☑00 from most other countries), Italy's country code (☑39) and then the area code of the location you want, including the leading 0.

→ The cheapest options for calling internationally are free or low-cost computer programs such as Skype, cut-rate call centres and international calling cards.

→ Cut-price call centres can be found in all of the main cities, and rates can be considerably lower than from Telecom payphones.

→ Another alternative is to use a direct-dialling service such as AT&T's USA Direct (access number ☑800 172444) or Telstra's Australia Direct (access number ☑800 172610), which allows you to make a reverse-charge (collect) call at home-country rates.

→ To make a reverse-charge international call from a public telephone, dial ☑170.

Mobile Phones (Cell Phones)

→ Italy uses GSM 900/1800, which is compatible with the rest of Europe and Australia but

---

Important Numbers

Italy country code (☑39)

International access code (☑00)

Police (☑113)

Carabinieri (military police; ☑112)

Ambulance (☑118)

Fire (☑115)

Roadside assistance (☑803 116 from a landline or mobile with an Italian provider; ☑800 116800 from a foreign mobile phone)

---

not with North American GSM 1900 or the totally different Japanese system.

→ Most smart phones are multiband, meaning that they are compatible with a variety of international networks. Check with your service provider to make sure it is compatible and beware of calls being routed internationally (very expensive for a 'local' call). In many cases you're better off buying an Italian phone or unlocking your phone for use with an Italian SIM card.

→ If you have a GSM multiband phone that you can unlock, it can cost as little as €10 to activate a prepaid SIM card in Italy. **TIM** (Telecom Italia Mobile; www.tim.it), **Wind** (www.wind.it) and **Vodafone** (www.vodafone.it) offer SIM cards and have retail outlets across Italy. You'll usually need your passport to open an account.

→ Once you're set up with a SIM card, you can easily purchase recharge cards (allowing you to top up your account with extra minutes) at tobacconists and news stands, as well as some bars, supermarkets and banks.

Payphones & Phonecards

→ You'll find payphones on the streets, in train stations and in Telecom offices. Most accept only *carte/schede telefoniche* (phonecards), although some accept credit cards.

→ Telecom offers a range of prepaid cards; for a full list, see www.telecomitalia.it/telefono/carte-telefoniche.

→ You can buy phonecards at post offices, tobacconists and news stands.

TOILETS

→ Public toilets are thin on the ground in Italy. You'll find them in autostrada service stations (generally free) and in main train stations (usually with a small fee of between €0.50 and €1).

→ Often, the best thing is to nip into a cafe or bar, although you'll probably have to order a quick drink first.

→ Keep some tissues to hand as loo paper is rare.

TOURIST INFORMATION

Practically every village, town and city in Italy has a tourist office of sorts. These operate under a variety of names: Azienda di Promozione Turistica (APT), Azienda Autonoma di Soggiorno e Turismo (AAST), Informazione e Assistenza ai Turisti (IAT) and Pro Loco. All deal directly with the public and most will respond to written and telephone requests for information.

Tourist offices can usually provide a city map, lists of hotels and information on the major sights. In larger towns and major tourist areas, English is usually spoken.

Main offices are generally open Monday to Friday; some also open on weekends, especially in urban areas and in peak summer season. Info booths (at train stations, for example) may keep slightly different hours.

Tourist Authorities
The **Italian National Tourist Office** (ENIT; www.enit.it) maintains international offices. See the website for contact details.

Regional tourist authorities are more concerned with planning, marketing and promotion than with offering a public information service. However, they offer useful websites:

Lombardy (www.turismo.regione.lombardia.it)

Piedmont (www.piemonteitalia.eu)

Trentino-Alto Adige (www.visittrentino.it, www.suedtirol.info)

Veneto (www.veneto.to)

Other useful websites include www.italia.it and www.easy-italia.com.

TRAVELLERS WITH DISABILITIES

Italy is not an easy country for travellers with disabilities. Cobbled streets, blocked pavements and tiny lifts cause problems for wheelchair users. Not a lot has been done to make life easier for the deaf or blind, either.

A handful of cities publish general guides on accessibility, among them Bologna, Milan, Padua (Padova), Reggio Emilia, Turin, Venice and Verona. Contact the relevant tourist authorities for further information. Other helpful resources:

Handy Turismo (www.handyturismo.it) Information on Rome.

Milano per Tutti (www.milanopertutti.it) Covers Milan.

Lonely Planet's free Accessible Travel guide can be downloaded here: http://lptravel.to/AccessibleTravel.

Useful organisations:

Accessible Italy (www.accessibleitaly.com) Specialises in holiday services for travellers with disabilities. This is the best first port of call.

Consorzio Cooperative Integrate (www.coinsociale.it) This Rome-based organisation provides information on the capital (including transport and access) and is happy to share its contacts throughout Italy. Its **Presidio del Lazio** (www.presidiolazio.it) program seeks to improve access for tourists with disabilities.

Tourism for All (www.tourismforall.org.uk) This UK-based group has information on hotels with access for guests with disabilities, where to hire equipment and tour operators dealing with travellers with disabilities.

VISAS

→ EU citizens do not need a visa for Italy.

→ Residents of 28 non-EU countries, including Australia, Brazil, Canada, Israel, Japan, New Zealand and the USA, do not require visas for tourist visits of up to 90 days.

→ Italy is one of the 15 signatories of the Schengen Convention. The standard tourist visa for a Schengen country is valid for 90 days. You must apply for it in your country of residence and you cannot apply for more than two in any 12-month period. They are not renewable within Italy.

→ For full details of Italy's visa requirements check www.esteri.it/visti/home_eng.asp.

Language

Italian sounds can all be found in English. If you read our coloured pronunciation guides as if they were English, you'll be understood. Note that ai is pronounced as in 'aisle', ay as in 'say', ow as in 'how', dz as the 'ds' in 'lids', and that r is strong and rolled. If the consonant is written as a double letter, it's pronounced a little stronger, eg *sonno son*·no (sleep) versus *sono so*·no (I am). The stressed syllables are indicated with italics.

BASICS

Hello.	*Buongiorno.*	bwon·*jor*·no
Goodbye.	*Arrivederci.*	a·ree·ve·*der*·chee
Yes./No.	*Sì./No.*	see/no
Excuse me.	*Mi scusi.*	mee *skoo*·zee
Sorry.	*Mi dispiace.*	mee dees·*pya*·che
Please.	*Per favore.*	per fa·*vo*·re
Thank you.	*Grazie.*	*gra*·tsye

You're welcome.
Prego. — *pre*·go

Do you speak English?
Parli inglese? — *par*·lee een·*gle*·ze

I don't understand.
Non capisco. — non ka·*pee*·sko

How much is this?
Quanto costa questo? — *kwan*·to *kos*·ta *kwe*·sto

ACCOMMODATION

Do you have a room?
Avete una camera? — a·*ve*·te *oo*·na *ka*·me·ra

How much is it per night/person?
Quanto costa per — *kwan*·to *kos*·ta per
una notte/persona? — *oo*·na *no*·te/per·*so*·na

DIRECTIONS

Where's ...?
Dov'è ...? — do·*ve* ...

Can you show me (on the map)?
Può mostrarmi — pwo mos·*trar*·mee
(sulla pianta)? — (*soo*·la *pyan*·ta)

EATING & DRINKING

What would you recommend?
Cosa mi consiglia? — *ko*·za mee kon·*see*·lya

I'd like ..., please.
Vorrei ..., per favore. — vo·*ray* ... per fa·*vo*·re

I don't eat (meat).
Non mangio (carne). — non *man*·jo (*kar*·ne)

Please bring the bill.
Mi porta il conto, — mee *por*·ta eel *kon*·to
per favore? — per fa·*vo*·re

EMERGENCIES

Help!
Aiuto! — a·*yoo*·to

I'm lost.
Mi sono perso/a. (m/f) — mee *so*·no per·*so*/a

I'm ill.
Mi sento male. — mee *sen*·to *ma*·le

Call the police!
Chiami la polizia! — *kya*·mee la po·lee·*tsee*·a

Call a doctor!
Chiami un medico! — *kya*·mee oon *me*·dee·ko

Want More?

For in-depth language information and handy phrases, check out Lonely Planet's *Italian Phrasebook*. You'll find it at **shop.lonelyplanet.com**, or you can buy Lonely Planet's iPhone phrasebooks at the Apple App Store.

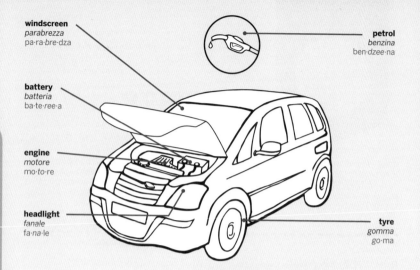

windscreen
parabrezza
pa·ra·bre·dza

petrol
benzina
ben·dzee·na

battery
batteria
ba·te·ree·a

engine
motore
mo·to·re

headlight
fanale
fa·na·le

tyre
gomma
go·ma

Signs

Alt	Stop
Dare la Precedenza	Give Way
Deviazione	Detour
Divieto di Accesso	No Entry
Entrata	Entrance
Pedaggio	Toll
Senso Unico	One Way
Uscita	Exit

ON THE ROAD

I'd like to hire a/an ...	Vorrei noleggiare ...	vo·ray no·le·ja·re ...
4WD	un fuoristrada	oon fwo·ree·stra·da
automatic/ manual	una macchina automatica/ manuale	oo·na ma·kee·na ow·to·ma·tee·ka/ ma·noo·a·le
motorbike	una moto	oo·na mo·to

How much is it ...?	Quanto costa ...?	kwan·to kos·ta ...
daily	al giorno	al jor·no
weekly	alla settimana	a·la se·tee·ma·na

Does that include insurance?
E' compresa l'assicurazione?
e kom·pre·sa la·see·koo·ra·tsyo·ne

Does that include mileage?
E' compreso il chilometraggio?
e kom·pre·so eel kee·lo·me·tra·jo

What's the city/country speed limit?
Qual'è il limite di velocità in città/campagna?
kwa·le eel lee·mee·te dee ve·lo·chee·ta een chee·ta/kam·pa·nya

Is this the road to (Venice)?
Questa strada porta a (Venezia)?
kwe·sta stra·da por·ta a (ve·ne·tsya)

(How long) Can I park here?
(Per quanto tempo) Posso parcheggiare qui?
(per kwan·to tem·po) po·so par·ke·ja·re kwee

Where's a service station?
Dov'è una stazione di servizio?
do·ve oo·na sta·tsyo·ne dee ser·vee·tsyo

Please fill it up.
Il pieno, per favore.
eel pye·no per fa·vo·re

I'd like (30) litres.
Vorrei (trenta) litri.
vo·ray (tren·ta) lee·tree

Please check the oil/water.
Può controllare l'olio/ l'acqua, per favore?
pwo kon·tro·la·re lo·lyo/ la·kwa per fa·vo·re

I need a mechanic.
Ho bisogno di un meccanico.
o bee·zo·nyo dee oon me·ka·nee·ko

The car/motorbike has broken down.
La macchina/moto si è guastata.
la ma·kee·na/mo·to see e gwas·ta·ta

I had an accident.
Ho avuto un incidente.
o a·voo·to oon een·chee·den·te

BEHIND THE SCENES

SEND US YOUR FEEDBACK

We love to hear from travellers – your comments help make our books better. We read every word, and we guarantee that your feedback goes straight to the authors. Visit **lonelyplanet. com/contact** to submit your updates and suggestions.

Note: We may edit, reproduce and incorporate your comments in Lonely Planet products such as guidebooks, websites and digital products, so let us know if you don't want your comments reproduced or your name acknowledged. For a copy of our privacy policy visit lonelyplanet.com/privacy.

ACKNOWLEDGMENTS

Climate map data adapted from Peel MC, Finlayson BL & McMahon TA (2007) 'Updated World Map of the Köppen-Geiger Climate Classification', *Hydrology and Earth System Sciences*, 11, 163344.

Cover photographs: Front: Lake Garda, HP Huber/4Corners ©; Back: Malcesine, Lake Garda, leoks/Shutterstock ©

THIS BOOK

This 1st edition of *Italian Lakes Road Trips* was researched and written by Cristian Bonetto, Belinda Dixon, Duncan Garwood, Paula Hardy and Donna Wheeler. This guidebook was produced by the following:

Destination Editor Anna Tyler

Product Editor Joel Cotterell

Senior Cartographers Valentina Kremenchutskaya, Anthony Phelan

Book Designer Wendy Wright

Assisting Editor Bruce Evans

Cover Researcher Naomi Parker

Thanks to Shahara Ahmed, Brendan Dempsey, Grace Dobell, Kate Kiely, Anne Mason, Darren O'Connell, Kirsten Rawlings, Victoria Smith, Angela Tinson, Tony Wheeler

OUR STORY

A beat-up old car, a few dollars in the pocket and a sense of adventure. In 1972 that's all Tony and Maureen Wheeler needed for the trip of a lifetime – across Europe and Asia overland to Australia. It took several months, and at the end – broke but inspired – they sat at their kitchen table writing and stapling together their first travel guide, *Across Asia on the Cheap*. Within a week they'd sold 1500 copies. Lonely Planet was born.

Today, Lonely Planet has offices in Melbourne, London and Oakland, with more than 600 staff and writers. We share Tony's belief that 'a great guidebook should do three things: inform, educate and amuse'.

INDEX

000 Map pages

Duncan Garwood Ever since moving to Italy in 1997, Duncan has spent much of his time driving the country on assignment for Lonely Planet. He's clocked up tens of thousands of kilometres and contributed to a whole host of Lonely Planet guidebooks, including *Italy, Rome, Sicily, Sardinia* and *Naples*, as well as the *Food Lover's Guide to the World*. He currently lives in the Castelli Romani hills just outside of Rome.

Paula Hardy From Lido beaches to annual Biennales and spritz-fuelled aperitivo bars, Paula has contributed to Lonely Planet Italian guides for over 15 years, including previous editions of *Venice & the Veneto, Pocket Milan, The Italian Lakes, Sicily, Sardinia* and *Puglia & Basilicata*. When she's not scooting around the *bel paese*, she writes for a variety of travel publications and websites. Currently she divides her time between London, Italy and Morocco, and tweets her finds @paula6hardy.

Donna Wheeler Italy's border regions are Donna Wheeler's dream assignment: Alps, the sea, complex histories, plus spectacular wine and food. Donna has lived in Turin's Quadrilatero Romano and Genova's centro storico and been an Italian-by-marriage for almost two decades. A former commissioning editor and content strategist, she's written guidebooks to Italy, France, Tunisia, Algeria, Norway and Belgium and publishes on art, architecture, history and food for LonelyPlanet.com, BBC.com Travel, National Geographic *Traveler* and My Art Guides; she is also the creative director of travel magazine *She Came to Stay*.

OUR WRITERS

Cristian Bonetto It took one visit to Italy as a young backpacker to get him hooked, and Cristian has been covering the country's food, culture and lifestyle for over a decade. The writer's musings have appeared in publications across the globe, and his Naples-based play *Il Cortile* (The Courtyard) has toured numerous Italian cities. Cristian has contributed to more than 30 Lonely Planet guides, including *Venice & The Veneto*, *New York City*, *Denmark*, and *Singapore*. You can follow Cristian's adventures on Twitter (@CristianBonetto) and on Instagram (rexcat75).

Belinda Dixon Having cut her travel teeth on Italy's ferries and trains, rarely has a year passed when Belinda hasn't been back. Research highlights include gazing at mountains while ferry-hopping those gorgeous lakes, encountering Mantua's extraordinary art, tasting olive oil in Malcesine and Bardolino in, well, Bardolino – and always delighting in this, the *bel paese*.

← **MORE WRITERS**

Published by Lonely Planet Publications Pty Ltd

ABN 36 005 607 983
1st edition – Jun 2016
ISBN 978 1 76034 053 7
© Lonely Planet 2016 Photographs © as indicated 2016
10 9 8 7 6 5 4 3 2 1
Printed in China

MIX
Paper from
responsible sources
FSC™ C021741
www.fsc.org

Paper in this book is certified against the Forest Stewardship Council™ standards. FSC™ promotes environmentally responsible, socially beneficial and economically viable management of the world's forests.